4th June 1998
Chicago

To Anty Kaul,
    R.S and
with good wishes!
        from —
    Toshi Pini.

ANATOMY
OF
CONSCIOUSNESS

ANATOMY
OF
CONSCIOUSNESS

By ISHWAR CHANDRA PURI

Published by
Ishwar Chandra Puri

Printed at Recorder Press, D-27, NDSE, Part-I, New Delhi.

This book is dedicated to my wife.

TO THE READER

TREMENDOUS is the word to describe human experience in its entirety. Even more so is the great Socratic theme—"KNOW THYSELF", the process that leads to self-realisation whereby we understand ourselves in the truest sense of the theme. It leads us to higher knowledge. It enables us to better understand other people and the world we live in.

Ishwar Chandra Puri has lectured in most parts of the world on a wide variety of such fascinating subjects as art, human awareness, human relations, morality, science, philosophy, religion, health and human consciousness, covering the entire scope of human experience. These lectures are so thorough and illuminating as to justify the title of this volume ("Anatomy of Consciousness") which is a summarisation of what he has said on the many facets of this deep, engrossing theme.

Going through the book from cover to cover one feels like being on an odyssey through the various stages of human consciousness. It is indeed a discovery—the discovery that the level of knowledge can be much higher than what exists within the reach of human mind. It becomes, therefore, a fascinating, if enigmatic, problem in philosophy, modern psychology and religion.

The vehicle of human consciousness, as it were, which remains beyond all intellectual comprehension, has been variously described as the soul, the mind, even the physical brain in some cases. There are aspects of this subject which can be studied and understood by anyone with an open mind and a sincere desire to get at the truth about one's own conscious experiences. But, there are higher aspects of it, relating to the very structure and mechanism of human consciousness. And only a trained intellect, aided by patience, sustained interest and systematic study, can comprehend the deepest mysteries of life.

The author attempts in these pages at providing an "intuitive glimpse" of the beauty and grandeur of this higher knowledge. And, taking a plunge, what does one find? From the Middle Ages to Renaissance to a new threshold, a kind of new evolution, viz., the evolution of human consciousness.

Man's material prosperity, attained through the ages, is undeniable. But, equally true is the fact that millions of people today are in quest of something beyond that, something higher than that. From science itself, as from the spiritual experiences of yogis and mystics, man is in the process of discovering a capacity in human consciousness for an awakening in a universe of endless mystery.

Love and logic have for long functioned independently of each other, leading to a "divided consciousness". The ANATOMY OF CONSCIOUSNESS is intended to give a description of what happens when one is able to explore the depths of one's own consciousness: a stage, that is, when a synthesis of intuition and reason, as of love and logic, has become possible.

CONTENTS

FOREWORD

I AM glad to have this opportunity to write a foreword to a commendable work on religion and philosophy, which will no doubt go a long way to foster and encourage the study of Human Awareness.

The search for truth, going on from time immemorial, will continue for all times to come. Truth is God. From the beginning the mind felt that truth was many-sided, and different views contained different aspects of truth, which no one could fully express. The Buddha insists that reason based on evidence is our only guide to truth. He asks us not to believe any sacred book merely because of its antiquity or regard for its author. Each one should search for himself, think for himself and realise for himself. Throughout one's life, living with one purpose, one has fought for truth and waged war against untruth, illustrating thus the endless quest of the mind, ever old, ever new.

In the past, world-weary men used to go out on pilgrimages to sacred places, mountains and forests to acquire inward peace, listening to the rush of winds and torrents, the music of birds and leaves, and returned full of heart and fresh in spirit. It was in the forest hermitages that the thinking men meditated on the deeper problems of existence. The search for truth still goes on, not as a kind of escapism but as a conscious endeavour on the part of a few enlightened men to reach the reality and make the task easier for the common man by showing the way to it.

We live in an age of hectic hurry, of deafening noise where most of us have no time or inclination for anything beyond the passing hour. True life grows within. It is in the inner solitude that a seeker finds his solace and where the quest has to be carried on. Yet, our modern life is unwilling to grant us this privilege. Not all of us, however, are deprived of this right, and if there is to be a creative movement some of us at least have to reflect on the problem so that we attain the ultimate reality and quench this thirst in those who are yearning to know something of it. Neither Plato nor Aristotle recommended a life of pure contemplation to a realized soul, though for both of them that was the best life. They directed wise men to serve the people.

We must realize that the truth which science or philosophy aims at is not of a provincial character. Its search may be conditioned, even restricted, by the mental attitudes and traditions of different countries, but we must aim at the universal truth. Even Western thinkers, shedding the provincial outlook, are admitting that thinkers outside their cultural traditions have grappled with the central problems of life.

The truth which claims to be universal requires to be continually re-created. It cannot be something already possessed, which needs only to be retransmitted. In every generation, it has to be renewed. Otherwise, it tends to become a dogma which induces complacency and does not encourage the supreme personal adventure. Tradition should be a principle, not of conservatism but of growth and regeneration. We cannot keep the rays of the sun while we put out the sun itself. Petrified tradition is a disease from which societies seldom recover. By the free use of reason and experience we appropriate truth and keep tradition in a continuous process of evolution. To have hold on people's minds, it must reckon with the vast reorientation of thought that has taken place. By re-interpreting the past, each generation stamps it with something of its own problems and pre-occupations. There are two levels of truth, the practical and the ultimate.

The study of classics, which are guardians of the past and heralds of the future, helps us to comprehend what is truth. It is dead if mechanically and unthinkingly accepted. It is alive if each generation *consciously* decides to receive it. Any system of thought should satisfy two basic requirements: it should state the truth and interpret it for each new generation. It must move back and forth between these two poles, the eternal and temporal. Truth is expressed in a human language formed by human thinking. The consciousness of this leads to a continual clarifying and fuller understanding of the truth.

The ultimate truths are truths of the spirit, and in the light of these the actual life has to be refined. Religion is hardly a dogma, but a working hypothesis of human conduct adapted to different stages of spiritual development and different conditions of life. Whenever it tends to crystallize itself in a fine creed, spiritual rituals and philosophic reactions are set up, which throw belief into the crucible of criticism, vindicating the true and combating the false. These are doubtless great moments in the history of thought, times of inward testing and vision when, at the summons of the spirit's breath, blowing where it listeth, and coming whence no one knows, the soul of man makes a fresh start and goes forth on a new venture. It is the intimate relation between the truth and the daily life of people that makes the quest always alive and real.

It is a moment of emotion, a great feeling of sincerity, which impels me to confess that my

hands tremble when I hold this book and remember the past. For, the author knows, and
knows so much, about my loves and hates for the
very mission that has now taken this form.

I wish all success to the author and hope
he continues his laudable work with zeal.

"The Voice Within"

INTRODUCTION

IT was some 20 years ago, during 1966-67, when, in connection with my research, I conceived the idea of writing. I kept on toying with the idea for long and could not do anything concrete until one evening in June 1982, when a friend transcribed a few tapes, and got a few books printed.

Joyous at this initial success, I took to this work more seriously.

'The incorrigible optimist' that I am, I attended more to action than to words of caution. For, people came to listen to me, and I have been amply rewarded. Luckily for me, there has been a very warm and encouraging response.

Believing in 'the breadth of vision' as the spirit of philosophy, I took care that the volume should not project or promote a single point of view but be a comprehensive conspectus that reflects all shades of opinion and, as such, mirrors the contemporary philosophic scene in its true colours. I wanted to, and happily can, compare it with an art gallery where work of all styles are exhibited, from the traditional to the modern, from the conformist to the nonconformist, from the graphic to the abstract, and so on. For, if we, e.g., begin with the 'soul' wherein it is maintained that the soul, like other natural existents, has evolved, that it is not only born and grows but can also decay and disintegrate, then we also have a view that the soul is external, unborn, immortal and indestructible.

I am quite sure that anybody who cares to turn the pages of this volume shall find something of interest to him or her.

Naturally, I am happy and proud of the fact that this labour of love has been brought to a successful culmination. Apparently, it is a one-man show, but I must, and do, realize that even a one-man show is not possible without countless number of persons toiling behind the scenes. I am fully aware that my own role has been nothing more than that of a Zero, the value of which is only because of the numbers going along with it. It is to that effect that I thankfully acknowledge the debt of gratitude that I owe to *"The voice within,"* who helped. I do not want to diminish my gratitude by mentioning names.

ISHWAR CHANDRA PURI
New Delhi 1986

Self-Realisation

I

SELF-REALIZATION

WHY did Socrates suggest that we should know our self? No one had ever suggested that one know one's self, because all knowledge is always of something else! A man may know millions and millions of things; he can become acquainted with the whole world, but if he is not aware of the "knower", he is still ignorant! He may become very knowledgeable but he will not become "wise". He may collect a lot of information and much knowledge, but the basic thing which makes one a "knower" is lacking—he is not aware of himself! But what, you may ask, is there to know about the self? It looks a little strange that this question should even be asked. People like Socrates are continually telling you to "know thyself" . . . but you do not want to know your self—you have already decided that you "KNOW" who you are. But do we really "know" what the "self" is? Even men with great philosophical and scientific insight are preplexed by this question. We are the self, what else is there to know about it? It seems very strange and even unnecessary that this question has continued to be asked for over 2,000 years. But it is a question still posed and still not fully answered! The most important question that mankind has ever encountered is "who am I?" But, it is a question which cannot be answered by anyone other than yourself. You have to look within your own self for the answer. You have to search; you have to become a seeker. It is a question which is absolutely private, and only you are capable of knowing the answer. It can only be answered through a deep inquiry into the core of your own being.

Today, there are thousands of philosophers, poets, yogis and so on who are still busy working on this problem of "knowing thyself". In Indian lore, there is a story of a man who went to a yogi and knocked at his door. The yogi said: "Who's there?" But there was no answer. There came a second knock and again the yogi asked: "Who's there?" Still there was no answer. The yogi shouted: "Why don't you say who you are?"—still no answer came! Third knock, the yogi screamed, "I said who are you? . . . what do you want?" The man answered, "If I knew that, I would not be knocking at your door! I have come precisely for the answer to this question." This is the case with us all. You are aware that, deep down within you, somehow YOU are missing . . . you exist but you don't know why; you don't know how; you don't even know WHO exists within you! You are somehow absent . . . you exist absently. You "exist", but you do not know what this "you" is. You do not "know thyself"! Man is unable to explain what he (himself) is, and this absence of "self-knowledge" has caused us to identify our self with the things we possess, instead of the "one" who possesses the thing. What is "mine" cannot be "me"! It is this false identification with what is "mine" but which could not possibly be "me", that creates all of our problems.

Whatever is mine cannot be me! If I say that this thing is mine, then it cannot be me! If I say that this jacket I am wearing is mine, then I clearly understand that the jacket is not me! When I assert that this jacket is mine, I am consciously aware of the fact that "I" am different from the jacket! That is why I call it "mine", and not "me".

2

I possess it, I own and use it, I wear it. It is **something** that belongs to me; something I carry around with me, but it cannot be me. This mine|me distinction must be clearly understood in order to fully grasp the extent of the fallacy we are making regarding what we are. We say that this body is mine, yet this body cannot be me! We say that these are my eyes, yet these eyes cannot be "me" either! We say that this is my mind yet the mind cannot possibly be "me"! "My" soul, "my" emotions, "my" this and "my" that—none of these things could possibly be "me", by the simple understanding of the mine|me distinction. Then what is the "me"? All that we have been identifying as the self belongs to us, but is actually not us. If it were, then we wouldn't call it "mine"—we would say it's "me"! What the "me" is, we have not been able to say yet. You have never encountered your self. You have never come face to face with your self—there has been no meeting. You simply "believe" you are this or that . . . that you are the things you have become identified with.

Whenever we have attempted to describe our "self", we have only been able to describe that which belongs to us. Therefore, if we ever want to understand what is the "me", we must first discover who is saying "this is mine". Who is claiming? Who is this claimant who is saying the body is "mine"; the mind is "mine", the soul is "mine". .who is claiming all this? If we can discover who this claimant is, we will be able to finally answer the question, "what is the self?" Therefore, let us examine what it is that is making these various claims—this house is mine, this family is mine, these children are mine, this body is mine and so on? It does not take very long to discover that it is "human consciousness" that is making all these claims! If we were not conscious and not human, no such claims could be made! If you were unconscious, you could never make all these claims. Therefore, the identity of the individual, who is continually

3

claiming that this or that is "mine", is linked directly and exclusively with his own consciousness! Without it, no claims can be made.

Human consciousness seems to provide the answer as to what the self is. Knowing this, you will "know thyself". In the journey towards knowing the self, all we have to do is to discover the nature of our "own" consciousness. How are we conscious? What makes us conscious..what makes us aware? Most people feel we are experiencing human awareness because we have a brain; that the phenomena of awareness and sensory perceptions are being generated by the human brain which, while we are alive, creates consciousness. But this is not entirely true.

There are many instances where, while alive, we do not experience awareness, and yet, the brain and the entire physical system remains functional! Examine the state of deep sleep. When we are in a state of deep sleep, our brain is there, the body and all of its support systems are still intact; we are alive and yet we are not CONSCIOUS! We do not experience awareness! If the experience of consciousness was merely based on the physical apparatus in the human body, then consciousness could not be shut off while the physical system is still! Moreover, even if it is the brain in the physical body that generated human consciousness, there are still many species of conscious experiences which cannot be attributed to it. Certain cases of extra-sensory perception, e.g., recall of previous lives (reincarnation), are clear instances of the functioning of consciousness outside of the data field available to the human brain and the physical system.

Leaving out these extra-sensory experiences going on in human consciousness, if we confine our examination to simply "non" wakeful experiences, we discover that we are still able to

4

have conscious perceptions which are not part of the physical system, i.e., dreams! Some dreams are so fantastic and bizarre that they cannot be traced to any experience or data picked up by the physical brain during the wakeful state of consciousness.

The perceptive apparatus of the physical body, which picks up experience via its sensory systems, receives impressions of the world around us, which in turn travel from the organs of perception, through the nervous system, and finally the brain picks up these messages. But it is ONLY WHEN WE ARE CONSCIOUS THAT THE BRAIN WILL PICK UP THESE IMPRESSIONS! Please make a note of this! If consciousness, which must casually precede experience, were not there the brain will not pick up any of the messages coming through the nervous system! If we are not conscious, the brain will not generate any response, even though it is functioning! Therefore, consciousness, per se, is the basis of perception and not the physical brain! However, the question what makes us conscious still remains unanswered.

The question of what causes us to be conscious is a question that we have all been asking ourselves for thousands of years, and still we have not found the answer. Our scientists have only been able to tell us which part of the brain EXPRESSES this or that aspect of consciousness. They are able, to some extent, to tell us which part of the brain is at work when we have audio or visual perceptions and so on, but what is actually causing conscious perception they cannot say! They have not, in spite of their elaborate equipment and labs, been able to find this out. They can only say that a certain part in the centre of the brain, which descends down into the medulla oblongata, into the spine, when choked off, shuts down most of our perceptive experiences. .but not all. You still retain some control over a few of the motor activities.

Therefore, our scientists cannot say that consciousness is controlled and generated by this part of the human brain; because it is not. In fact, our scientists still have very limited information on what constitutes consciousness. They still do not know what makes a man conscious. But it has become obvious, especially to scientists working in this field, that what enables us to be conscious is not something that is material. Yet it does seem to be embodied in matter, in the physical brain or in this physical body somewhere. But somehow or the other, we are still capable of having conscious experiences outside of the domain and field of data available to the physical system, i.e., certain types of dreams.

In certain dreams, people have dreamt that they were a little bird and that they flew out of a window and so on. They "personally" experienced being a bird! I am taking this kind of dream simply as an example of a "non" wakeful conscious experience and not for any other reason. Don't give it too much importance. But suppose you were to go to sleep and have this kind of a dream in which you are a bird. You become a bird and fly out of the window. You will then have the conscious experience of BEING a bird. . that you were actually a bird! Upon awakening, naturally you will discover that you are not a bird, but a human being with a human body. You realize that you don't have feathers, that you don't have wings and so on, and that you cannot fly! There is no resemblance between the bird and yourself. But still you do not say, "In my dream 'I SAW A BIRD THAT FLEW OUT OF A WINDOW'!" You will say, "I WAS a bird and I flew out of the window!" The experience retained the personal self. It retains your own human consciousness, and if you say to a friend that last night you dreamt that you were a bird flying all around, your friend will say that this is simply nonsense! There is no resemblance

6

between you and a bird. Just say that you "saw" a bird flying in your dream last night, otherwise people will think you are either stupid or have gone mad! But you will say, NO! I didn't "see" a bird. .I wasn't looking at some bird flying out of a window, I "WAS" A BIRD! I never "saw" it! I flew! I was flying! It is the retention of the identity of being the SAME conscious experiencer when awake, whose body became that of a bird which compels you to make this claim! Here is a conscious experience quite outside of the physical body.

Human consciousness is thus capable of having awareness, in the form of a bird or otherwise, and can generate an experience of the world around it. Even "dream" bodies, which are bodies different from the human body with which we have identified ourselves, are also assumed to be the origin of human consciousness. In a dream, consciousness functions in a different form from this physical body. We walk around all over and come back to this form only when we awaken.

Consciousness, the capacity of the human self to have awareness and generate conscious experiences of the world around it, could not possibly be generated by the physical body or any part of it, i.e., the physical brain. Therefore, no wonder we say that this is "my" body, and that it is not "me"! It is just proper that we say this, because "me" is the consciousness that claims that this body is used by it; that it belongs to me—I just function through it! What, then, is consciousness, without the physical body, without a dream body and so on, like? The practitioners of the art of self-realization, based on their own personal experiences, have constructed a very simple model of the structure and anatomy of human consciousness.

7

II

▼

WHAT IS CONSCIOUSNESS

BEFORE we examine the nature and structure of human consciousness, I would like to define a few terms that I will be using in the discussion of this subject. They have been used so loosely and with so many different meanings that one can easily become confused. These terms have been used by so many different minds, different backgrounds and conditioning that they are bound to have different meanings to you. Even in ordinary conversation, when one says something, one says it with one meaning. When it reaches the other person, he gives a different meaning to those same words. When this is the case with ordinary conversation, imagine the problem that arises when we discuss a subject as subtle as this. Understanding the meaning of these terms will enable us to avoid many problems arising from semantics and will enable the reader at once, to clearly understand exactly what I will be explaining. The terms that I would like to define are: consciousness, awareness, attention, subconsciousness, superconsciousness, unconsciousness and "psychic" energy forces. These are all terms which I will be frequently using. Therefore, it will be useful to know what they mean. This will facilitate the transfer of a great deal of knowledge about the anatomy of human consciousness.

I am using the word consciousness in a much larger sense than it is commonly used. Consciousness is the possibility, the potential to be conscious, the compulsion to be conscious. It is the everlasting experience of being conscious. It needs no fuel; it needs no rest. It is pure energy. . perpetual internal energy! It is the totality of potential awareness. . . . the capacity to be conscious. Consciousness. . . . is not merely the capacity to be conscious at a particular moment, but it also includes the potential and possibility to be conscious at any given moment throughout the entire domain of the time-space continuum! Consciousness includes the potential to be conscious of the past as well as of the future! It even includes the capacity to be conscious of those experiences which occur OUTSIDE of the time-space continuum!

Consciousness, they say, is the totality of our capacity to have conscious experiences per se, whether we are immediately aware of it or not! Consciousness includes the conscious awareness of a contemporary experience, as well as the potential capacity to be aware of any experience—whether within the time-space complex or outside of it. On the other hand, awareness represents that region of consciousness of which we are conscious at any given time.

Awareness is the "present" field of consciousness—what we are now (immediately) conscious of. It is our "available" consciousness. Out of the totality of consciousness, something is flowing through time into immediate consciousness. . into awareness. This does not simply include that which is being perceived through the sensory system. . . . what we are now seeing, hearing, tasting and so on. It also includes the things you are not seeing or hearing, but have the potential to hear, see and so on. Those things which you can become aware of whenever you want to; which are "available"

9

in the same time frame—these belong to the scope and domain of "awareness".

Attention is a probe, a narrowed down beam of awareness, which is focussed onto a particular area in the domain of the immediate conscious experiences available to us. Attention is that part of awareness within which we are moving around inside the domain of our possible experience, in order to become "more" aware of a certain part of it, to give it a greater significance in consciousness; to become "consciously aware" of it. Therefore, attention is simply that part of awareness which we use to focus our consciousness upon something. For example, the whole room you are sitting in is a part of your awareness—now.

But, your "attention" is on this book, this particular page and line . . . . this particular word! Therefore, your attention is picking up only a part of the "available" awareness in the room in which you are sitting! You can pick up other parts also, by shifting and manipulating your attention from one thing to another. Whenever the attention is shifted from one object to another, you will be picking up certain parts in your field of immediate awareness, in order to have a closer look at them. Human attention is that faculty in consciousness which enables us to have this deeper experience of any part of the domain of our awareness. Human attention also performs another function in human consciousness. It also enables us to become LESS aware of a certain part of our experience! It's a double-edged sword, which cuts both ways. It can increase your power to be conscious of a thing, and at the same time it enables you to cut off the awareness of whatever you do not wish to experience! Later, you will see how this second feature of attention is even more important than the first.

Subconsciousness is a storage area. It is that part of consciousness in which our memories are stored. It is that area of consciousness which lies outside the field of our immediate awareness. Subconsciousness is that part of consciousness of which we are unaware by virtue of "forgetfulness"; by virtue of the shutting down or inhibiting of the memory process. But it can be regained and brought back into the field of our immediate awareness when we turn on memory process.

Unconsciousness is simply another name for subconsciousness. It is a more modern term and is used more frequently than subconsciousness because subconsciousness is not really a "part" of awareness—we have actually forgotten it. Therefore, the word "unconsciousness" has been preferred, but there is no real difference between the two of them.

Superconsciousness is the capacity to bring into awareness the level of consciousness lying outside the field of our immediate awareness through a process of "expanding" awareness! Thus, the distinction between subconsciousness or unconsciousness and superconsciousness or unconsciousness and superconsciousness would be that subconsciousness can be brought into the field of awareness by the use of MEMORY—whereas, superconsciousness is brought into the field of awareness by the technique of expanding awareness . . . often referred to as meditation.

"Psychic" energy force is the flow of "currents" of consciousness coming through the centres of the physical body, from beyond the scope and domain of awareness. "Psychic" energy flow is that part of consciousness which operates through energy centres in the physical vehicle of the human body. It enables the experience to flow outwards, as well as inwards. It enables an experience to be "objective" or "subjective" . . . or both! The physical body has a continuous flow of conscious energy, of consciousness, travelling through

11

all of its parts! This energy flows out, from the body into our experiences lying within the domain of awareness. It flows out through sense perceptions. It then sustains these physical experiences, and makes them a close circuit experience. This energy flows through the human body from fixed centres, which then function as the focal points for the flow of consciousness throughout our physicality!

Having defined these terms, it now becomes clear that when we speak of levels of consciousness, we are not merely speaking of levels of awareness, but, more fundamentally, we are speaking of levels of "possible" awareness—levels of potential awareness.

A higher level of consciousness is qualitatively different from a higher level of awareness, and is not merely "knowing" more about the world around us. I am making this point because very often students of awareness, and even practitioners of the art of meditation, make the mistake of regarding expansion of awareness as raising the level of consciousness. One can know a great deal about this world by increasing awareness but it would not mean he has attained a higher level of consciousness. For example, suppose you are now aware of the room you are sitting in, but not aware of the rest of the world around you. You then decide to become aware of it by "raising" your level of consciousness through some particular technique or meditational practice. Actually, the level of consciousness you have "attained" remains the same as before. It is the same level of consciousness at which, initially, only the room was in awareness, afterwards more of the world came into awareness. The rest of the world comes into awareness—this is all that has happened! This kind of "expanding" of one's awareness does not lead to any "higher" level of consciousness. One has simply expanded one's "awareness" at the SAME level of consciousness! Yet, there are hundreds of students and practitioners of the art of meditation, who go on thinking that since something more has come into their immediate field of awareness, they have, in fact, reached a higher level of consciousness. This, however, is not true. What then are these higher levels of consciousness?

These higher levels of consciousness are related to our concepts, at any given moment, of what the "self" is! When we regard this physical body as our own self, then we are in the "physical" level of consciousness! All of the awareness that comes to us about the physical world, about anything that is happening on earth, in this physical universe, would constitute degrees of awareness within a single level of human consciousness called the "physical" level of consciousness. This physical level of consciousness would represent our "wakeful" state, that is the state of consciousness you are now in. The state in which you are reading this book. This state is called the "wakeful" state of physical consciousness. This is considered one of the lowest levels of human consciousness. If, while in this state of consciousness, you happen to have a number of weird or bizarre experiences, it would not constitute a change in your level of consciousness. They would only be different experiences. They may be different degrees of awareness, but the level of consciousness would be the same, i.e., the physical "wakeful" level of consciousness.

When you go to sleep and have a dream, then this "dream state" would constitute a still lower level of consciousness! Why lower? Why not different? Because, in the dream state, you do not even use the physical body at all. You use a "dream" body, which is different, more ethereal, and which has been created only for the purpose of that particular dream. It is the dream body alone which senses and experiences the dream world. Therefore, the "dream state" is a lower level of consciousness. It is sustained by a dream body, by an "imaginary" body that you have

13

created yourself through the mental process of dreaming! Another reason why we consider the dream level of consciousness to be a lower level of consciousness is because the dream level is always "sandwiched" between two wakeful states of consciousness! When we are "awake", we can shut off this wakeful state of consciousness by going to sleep; by merely becoming "unconscious" of our physical body! When we relax and shut off the awareness of our physical body, we move into the dream state automatically! But it is an experience of a very short duration, followed by a much longer state of wakefulness.

In a long wakeful state, a lifetime lasting many years between birth and death, we have many experiences of these short dream sequences, which are lower levels of consciousness. While we are asleep, we become unconscious of our body, and then a dream sequence starts. But when we wake up we not only get back the consciousness of our body, we also realize that we were always in this world, even while asleep! This realization, that we were in this world all the time, makes the dream a lower level of consciousness. The knowledge that the body in which we have slept; the body which was lying on the bed before and is still lying on the bed when we wake up, is all that is necessary to convince us that we were asleep. We don't have to open our eyes; we don't have to pinch ourselves to see if we are awake. All that is required is that we remember we went to sleep. The fact that we retain the continuity of the physical experience preceding the dream state proves that this "wakeful" state is more real!

The immediate recall of our earlier state of physical wakeful consciousness, upon awakening, gives us certain proof that the dream state was only temporary, and not "real", and whenever we have an experience of a higher level of consciousness than this wakeful state, a similar change must also take place. It must be a kind of "awakening" into another kind of body, not this one, which we discover was existing throughout the duration of the "wakeful sequence"— a body of which we had become temporarily unconscious! Then, and then alone, can we say that we have raised our level of consciousness to a higher level!

When one examines the different experiences which have been regarded as superconscious experiences, one will find that many of these experiences are dream-like—one feels that the person must be having some weird or fantastic dream, and is wrongly calling it a "higher" level of consciousness. You may be a very wise and learned dreamer; you can be very knowledgeable in your dream, but a dreamer is a dreamer. You can dream of very beautiful sights and scenes of golden temples and sweet music ... even of heaven, but no dream, however, beautiful it may be, however great it may look, could ever be a higher level of consciousness, unless it results in a "higher" state of wakefulness. If it does not provide us with a body, in which we have consciousness over a much longer period of time than in this physical body, it is not a higher level of consciousness! When you attain a real and truly higher level of consciousness, you will wake up into a different body which exists at that level of consciousness; which has been with you all the time! It was there, even while you were having this physical experience. This, then, is a very easy test to apply. Many yogic states, which are misunderstood to be higher levels of consciousness, are merely different levels of awareness contained in the "same" level of consciousness, namely, the wakeful level. Very often, these trances which yogis can attain are trances induced by a type of "sleep" in which the dream episode is regulated. But a dream is a dream, however regulated it may be! It is "maya", an illusion, the "stuff" of which dreams are made. These so-called "inner" experiences may be

15

unusual, and perhaps even beautiful, but they are mistakenly being called superconscious experiences—experiences of a higher level of consciousness.

Most of them will be found not to be experiences of a higher level of consciousness, or a different awareness at the same level of consciousness. When a higher level of consciousness is experienced, your will have the sensation of waking up from a dream! You will recall, in your own memory, the point of time when you fell "asleep" into this lower wakeful state of consciousness. Unless this recall comes, you cannot be sure of having had an experience of a higher level of consciousness.

When we wake up from a dream, we don't pinch ourselves, we don't ask questions and so on. No proof is required! Every morning you wake up, every night you go to sleep. But you never go about asking people if you are awake or still dreaming! You never do this. You are CERTAIN that you are awake. What makes you so certain? It is the recall, the memory of the fact that you went to sleep! If you did not remember that you had gone to sleep, you would never be sure that the intervening experience was a dream. In other words, to have a dream, you must first be awake! In the same way, in order to have a higher experience than this wakeful level of consciousness, there must be the recall of a higher level of consciousness from which we had earlier descended, (in a dream-like way), into this present wakeful level of consciousness! When we rise back to that higher level of consciousness, the experience should be identical to that of waking up from a dream. We should be able to recall when we went into this lower state of physical wakeful consciousness. It is precisely this kind of proof that comes to those who are able to truly shift their level of consciousness one step above this physical level of consciousness, to what is called—the "astral" level of consciousness.

What happens when you shift the level of consciousness one step up to the astral level? When this is done, the reverse of what happens when you go into the dream state takes place. When you go into the dream state you merely pick up a few of the perceptions from the wakeful state and rejumble them into a less coherent, less consistent framework of rules and laws and we then have an experience within this framework. In the present state of wakeful consciousness we experience everything in a regulated time frame. Todays follow yesterdays and tomorrows follow todays. However, in a dream, this need not happen. Todays can be followed by yesterdays and so on, and it will not bother you in a dream. Time gets all jumbled up, flows backwards, discontinuously. Yet never do such dream experiences seem unusual. While in that state of consciousness, it looks odd and even queer, but we still regard those events as REAL! In a dream, we often do some of the most bizarre things. We can defy all the laws of nature pertaining to the wakeful experience; yet they are accepted as natural and real while the dream lasts. In the wakeful state we must follow the laws of gravity. However, in a dream, we may walk on the ceiling and it would not bother us! We carry people from the wakeful state and, in our dream, we jumble up their relationships to us and to each other. Your wife may be your daughter in a dream or your boss becomes your son and so on, and yet these jumbled-up roles seem quite real to us while we are in the dream state.

It is only when we shift our consciousness, to the higher wakeful state of consciousness, do we see the "higher reality" on which the dream had been based. Similarly, this whole world is like a dream and has a higher reality than we can see at this level of physical, wakeful consciousness. Just look around you. Watch the people you are around, look at their faces. Notice how they are moving about. Watch their

17

gestures, and so on. A few are simply talking to themselves, no one is really listening to anyone. Their lips are just moving, they themselves don't even know what they are saying! Everyone seems to be in a dream; in a world of his own—that is why there is so much conflict and friction.

Each person is living in his or her own dream world, so that whenever two persons come close, friction occurs, sooner or later. It is bound to happen because their "dreams" cannot coincide—and everybody wants to impose his dream upon the other. This is the problem, because you cannot interpose your dream with another person. You cannot share it with others. You cannot force your husband or wife to "see things your way"! He or she is dreaming, and so are you! And dreaming is such a private phenomenon that you become completely unaware of the "real" world which surrounds you. This reality can be "seen" at the next higher level of consciousness....the "astral" level of consciousness!

III

THE ASTRAL LEVEL

A T the astral level, the same people we know at this wakeful level of consciousness are seen in a much more "real" sense. At this physical level of consciousness, we are having a distorted experience and, therefore, people appear to be doing stupid and foolish things. But, this is a lower level of consciousness, and if we could see these same people from a higher level of consciousness, they would be seen to be far more consistent, far more beautiful and wise, than now. This foolishness that we are seeing in them at this physical level of awareness is a distortion of their "higher reality" taken from the higher (astral) level of consciousness!

At the astral level of consciousness, everyone is more beautiful, more intelligent and wise; events are much more consistent. Individuals who have experienced this higher astral level of consciousness, who have "awakened" into this higher level, recall that they were here before going into this "dream-like" wakeful state. And they have described the experience as a very beautiful one: an experience in which they were able to see the light and the beauty in all things and in all people. People who look so ugly at the physical level of consciousness are seen to be really radiant and beautiful from the astral level. They have light glowing around them! Even nature is seen to be much more beauti-

19

ful than ordinarily conceivable at a lower level of consciousness. The astral experience is "aesthetically" superior to anything that we know of at this level. Even in terms of our non-sensual experiences, everything is very different!

At the astral level of consciousness, it is no longer necessary to use words in order to communicate! The method of communication used by those who have awakened to the astral level of consciousness is telepathic. They simply think out something and the other person knows what is being thought! The normal means of communication at the astral level is telepathy, although at this level of consciousness one can also use speech, if one so desires. Words are used merely to add beauty to communication. Everything connected with this higher astral level of consciousness is superior, especially the amount of knowledge we are able to pick up. There is a storehouse of knowledge there which is based on the work done by the "astral conscious" people for billions of years! Here, at the physical level of consciousness, we go to a university or library and select a particular subject to know more about it. We read various books on physics, chemistry, etc., and we are then able to benefit from the history of the scientific research done in these fields. If we want, we can do experiments to build upon the work already done in certain areas. Similarly, at the astral level of consciousness, we are able to do the same thing. . . . with one big difference.

If you are interested in a particular subject, you go to the "AKASHIC" libraries and there, not only will you be able to study what HAS been done, but also what WILL be done on earth for the next 2,000 years! It is a different kind of learning experience. People who have been able to get into this higher level of consciousness are collecting immense knowledge in those libraries. Knowledge, which can be verified again and again, is available there. Not only is the knowledge available at this level much greater, but the whole concept of time and space is also different there!

At the astral level of consciousness, we are able to travel huge distances to any part of space. There, we are not bound by the velocity or the speed of light as we are here! At this physical level of consciousness, our sensory perceptions are confined to this physical body and the various mechanical means of locomotion devised for its use. None of these are able to travel faster than the velocity of light. And because of the relatively low velocity at which we are able to travel, our experience gets restricted to a very, very limited area of space. Scientists have very recently dis-covered quasars travelling at velocities greater than the velocity of light, at the fringes of space. Beyond the velocity of light, there exists an immense space, completely inaccess-ible to anything which cannot exceed the velocity of light! At this lower physical level, because we move far below the velocity of light, we can never cross over to have any experience in this part of space.

We can "transcend" the speed of light. We are actually able to have locomotion—to have mobility at much "higher" velocities than light. . . . over much greater distances than the distances available to the physical body. Therefore, the space which we have for travel is correspondingly much greater at the astral level. A trip even to the very fringes of space, as we know it, would be nothing compared with the trips one can make at the astral level of consciousness! This is an experi-ence which anyone can have, by shifting to the higher "astral" level of consciousness. This is not simply a theoreti-cal possibility. It is a practical possibility as well. All that is required is the "raising" of consciousness one step above this present wakeful state. When this is done we discover that we have the capacity to see better, to com-municate better, to hear better. . . . the capacity to do every-

21

thing with the senses better, at the astral level of consciousness. All of these capacities lie dormant in human consciousness.

The question naturally arises as to what facilities are available to us for such "astral" travel and experience. We use what is called the "astral" body. It is our "vehicle" for experiences at the astral level of consciousness. The "astral" body is nothing more than the "pure" form of the sensory perceptions that are locked up in this physical body! It is the gross material out of which this physical vehicle of human consciousness is constructed that limits our movement. When we want to go somewhere, what keeps us from going there directly and immediately? It is the physical body! You have to carry it with you. If you did not have to carry it, you could go anywhere you want anytime, and AT ONCE! What prevents you from flying out of your window right now and taking a trip around the city? The world? It is the physical body! It would fall down and be broken to pieces if you tried to fly out of your window right now! If you could somehow be relieved of the grossness of the physical body, you will find that there is nothing in your sensory system of perception preventing you from having the entire experience of this world. . . . of the universe! The astral body, which enables us to have this "astral" experience, is being carried by, or is locked up within, us all the time!

In fact our sensory experiences—even while functioning with this physical body—are arising from the astral body (which exists inside the physical body)! If this astral body were to cease, even just for a second, this physical body would become simply a lump of dead clay! We would have no feeling left in it! All the feelings, all the senses, all the perceptions experienced through the physical body are arising from the presence of the astral body residing within the physical body. Our sensory system exists per se, and is

22

entirely independent of this physical body. So, when we are able to free the operating of our sensory system from the restriction of the physical body, we regain the capacity in consciousness to function entirely free from the limitations of time and space! This experience is often referred to as "astral projection", or "astral travel", because it is with the astral body that we are able to have these kinds of beautiful experiences.

The astral body shines and glows and has a shape very much like that of this physical body. It has hands and feet with which it moves from place to place. This astral body does precisely the same thing that is done by the physical body, except that it functions with infinitely greater speed, beauty and efficiency! Only those who have had the astral experience are able to know how beautiful it is. I don't know why I am even trying to describe it in words. I am just trying to convince you that it is a superior state of consciousness, by highlighting some of the features of the astral experience. We were all in this "astral form" before we were born! Birth is merely the process of falling asleep into this physical level of consciousness. What we are considering as a lifetime is nothing more than a dream arising from the astral level of consciousness, and at the time of what we call death the astral body "awakes". We will then recall that we had simply fallen asleep! The entire set of memories from the previous life we led, prior to birth, comes back into our recollection and we can see them! When we are able to have the astral experience now....to "DIE WHILE LIVING"....we are then able to explain many things that we otherwise were not able to comprehend. For example, we meet many people whom we dislike at first sight. We don't know why, because they have never done anything to harm or hurt us. At the astral level of consciousness, we are able to see exactly WHY! We are able to see the nature of our relationship with that person at this higher level of reality, and how this "reality" has been reflected, to some extent, at the lower level of physical consciousness.

At the astral level, we see what they did to us and what we have done to them. We come to realize that it was a lesson learned from this previous astral episode, which now causes us to dislike a certain person, for no "apparent" reason, at this lower level of consciousness. Also, we meet people whom we immediately like. Why? The same reason! There are some places we go to and feel we have been there before. What is referred to as "deja vu", the feeling of having "seen" it all before. Yet, physically speaking, we know that we have never been there before! When we "awake" to the higher astral level of consciousness, we are able to recall precisely when we saw that place or thing for the first time. It was seen in an earlier episode from the previous life, before we slept into this physical level of consciousness. These are just a few of the experiences we all have had which convince us of not only a higher level of consciousness, but also give us an insight into many other perplexing experiences which we are unable to explain. The astral level of consciousness is only one step above in the hierarchy of levels of human consciousness. There are possibilities of raising levels of consciousness far above this. What would be the next step?

Above the astral level of consciousness, there is another level of consciousness which we call the "mental" or "causal" level of consciousness. When we awake further from the astral level of consciousness to the causal level, we are then able to see people in their pure mental forms. We no longer are restricted to seeing them in the categories of sense perceptions. At this causal level of consciousness, we no longer communicate with each other by telepathy, but by direct perception! Direct perception is entirely different from telepathy! With telepathy, one says something in one's own mind, and then the other person listens with his mind.

In direct perception, you don't say anything! The other person, who has also attained causal consciousness, already "KNOWS" your thoughts. It is what we call "transference" of understanding. It is a common experience at the causal level of consciousness to communicate through the transference of understanding. The recollection of memories that we regain at the causal level of consciousness goes back to the very beginning of time! To the very first instance of time, whenever that was. And, our knowledge moves onwards to the very edge of time, whatever that means. At this causal level of consciousness, we are able to see that in the astral experience we merely picked up a part of this causal experience, confined it to a certain time frame and went through it like a dream. And then, some part of this astral experience was picked up in the physical level of consciousness, and projected upon the screen of this physical world where we experienced it! In the causal level of consciousness—the "pure" mental level of consciousness—it is not just this mind sitting in this physical body, but the actual "shifting" of our level of consciousness, and our experiences are far more beautiful. Our knowledge greatly transcends that of the astral level!

When we are able to awake further from the astral level of consciousness, through an actual process of wakefulness. . . . when this takes place, we gain access to all that has ever happened and all that will ever happen to us! Not only to us personally, but to anybody. . . . anywhere in the world! We regain a universal memory, a universal mind, a universal repository of experience which is available to us at this causal level of consciousness. It is difficult to describe the beauty and immensity of knowledge flowing at this level of human consciousness! The entire "universal mind", the single mind which operates through millions and billions of individual minds at the lower levels of consciousness, is available to us at the causal level of human consciousness! Through the causal mind we can know the entire content of all the individual minds that exist or that will ever exist! The experience and knowledge accessible to the causal or universal mind is so immense; the beauty of this experience is so tremendous, that there is no parallel to it at the lower levels of astral and physical consciousness! It is a remarkable experience.

The experience of knowing the contents of all minds, at once, is so unique and so unusual, that there is no possibility of any dream-like yogic experience ever being compared to it. Causal consciousness is a much higher experience than these lower "astral" experiences. When we are able to reach the causal level of consciousness, we are able to have experience through "pure" mind, without the restriction of the grosser astral body. The astral body is as restrictive and gross upon the causal self as the physical body is upon the astral self! At the astral level, we discover that we had been unable to do or go where we wish because of this physical body.

Similarly, at the causal level, we discover that the astral body itself prevents us from having immediate and complete experiences! All of our astral experiences are divided into the various categories of sensory perception, i.e., seeing, tasting, smelling and so on. We are limited to the experiencing of the "whole" through its parts. Astral consciousness provides us only with "partial" experiences of reality! Human attention plays an important role in all astral perceptions and the narrow scope of attention restricts and limits our experiences. We are only able to have a "part by part" regulated awareness of an experience . . . . never the direct, simultaneous experience of the whole! At the causal level, that is the third and next higher level of consciousness above the astral level, you become "one" with the entire "mind" of all mankind . . . the universal mind! You are able to "know" directly, and not part by part, the entire experience undergone by all minds, throughout the whole history of mankind, as well as all the future experiences of mankind! It is a tremendous experience, and there has been no way, for those who have attained this level of consciousness, to describe it!

Even those who have just heard about it, and have tried to describe it could only say, "neti, neti"—not this, not that! They said there is no way to describe it. How can you describe an experience in which the totality of the human mind can be experienced all at one time? The causal experience, the level of the universality of mind, has truly been described by the practitioners of the art of meditation as the attainment of "God-realization". Of having FOUND God! God-consciousness has been equated to the consciousness of universal mind. The consciousness of what is called the "Brahma" in India. . . . the Creator. At this causal level of consciousness, man becomes "one" with God. At this level of consciousness, all the knowledge that exists, or could ever exist, is known! One becomes "OMNISCIENT"! Everything that can ever happen in time and space becomes knowable at the causal level of human consciousness!

All "beginnings" exist at this level of consciousness. The beginning of every event occurring in time and space exists at this level! All "middles" and all "endings" of these events are also included here! Everything that has ever happened, or will ever happen within the time-space-causation framework, lies here at the causal level in human consciousness! It is one of the most beautiful experiences available in human consciousness! And all of this is attained by awakening from the astral level of consciousness by an actual, wilful and deliberate experience of "wakefulness" . . . of waking up from the astral level of consciousness. When this happens, we are

27

able to recall the previous state of consciousness we had before sleeping in the astral level of consciousness. The whole of our memory comes back to us! The total memory of all mankind comes back to us, and we recall how this total experience was split up into various segments, in order to sustain the dream sequences below. The totality of all possible experience is stored at this causal level of consciousness.

So much having been said about this causal level, you are probably presuming that there can be no higher level of consciousness beyond this! At this level everything is included... even God. Therefore, many practitioners of religion, yoga, meditation and so on have taken it as the last and the highest state of consciousness. They have said that this is the ultimate level of consciousness. When one has reached the region of universal mind, what else could there be beyond it? What else could there be beyond time, space and causation? And yet, I say, there is still a level of consciousness beyond this causal level of consciousness! This is the level beyond the mind, which is called the level of "pure spiritual consciousness".

IV

THE MIND—AND THE SOUL

WHAT, then, would this fourth level of consciousness beyond the mind, beyond time, space and causation be like? Whatever I have described up to this point—the totality of human experience—all takes place in time, space and causality. Everything that is there at the level of causal consciousness, universal mind, universal memory, universal experience ...all these experiences, even if universal, are locked within the framework of time, space and causation! This totality of experience is confined to the time-space continuum. The level of pure "spiritual" consciousness lies beyond time-space and causation.

At this level of consciousness one is able to experience the pure soul! It is the experience of pure human consciousness, without any restriction from the mind from the time, space and causation framework. Please note that the mind is not material, not something that exists per se. This must be clearly understood. When human consciousness operates within this time-space-causality framework, it is called the mind. The mind is merely a term which connotes the behaviour of human consciousness as it operates within this continuum. At the pure spiritual level of consciousness, the restriction of time, space and causation does not come in the way of the freedom of human consciousness.

We have noticed how, at each of the lower levels of consciousness, there was always something which inhibited and restricted the functioning of the next higher level of consciousness. In the dream state, below the physical wakeful state of consciousness, the jumbled rules and laws of nature restricted our freedom of experience. In the wakeful state, the physical level of consciousness, the gross physical body restricted our freedom and range of experience. At the astral level of consciousness, the sensory system and its division of perception into senses restricted our freedom. And at the causal level of consciousness, it is time-space and causation which restricts the freedom of our conscious experiences.

But, when we rise to the level of the human soul, to the level of pure spiritual consciousness, we are able to have conscious experiences unfettered and unrestricted by any of these things! We discover that we are pure, intuitive souls! Pure, intuitive, conscious beings, not restricted by any laws, any bodies, any division of perception or any time, space and causality! We don't need bodies, we don't need the mind or any of these apparatuses in order to have conscious experiences. At this "intuitive" level of consciousness, we discover that these were simply encumbrances upon consciousness! They were not aids. We discover that, in fact, they were cages in which consciousness had been locked.

At the pure spiritual level of consciousness, we regain an awareness that transcends the collected awareness of all the levels of consciousness below it! In Indian terminology, they could find no other way to describe this experience except by the word..."par-brahma"—that which is beyond the "brahma", the Creator! Since the universal consciousness available at the causal level of consciousness has been considered as the level of the Creator, this state of

30

pure spiritual consciousness has been called par-brahma...
beyond the Creator.

Therefore, you can imagine from what has been said so far how difficult it would be to describe that state of consciousness in which a person can experience that which is beyond the Creator! When we say that "In the beginning, there was God and he created the heavens....", we are referring to the Brahma, the creator of all that came into existence AFTER time! Because the "beginning" was there before the creator. If, in the beginning the creator did this and that, then there was a "time flow" even before the creator! He had to start from the beginning! Who created time? Who created the beginning? Who was beyond beginning... beyond the creator?

The human mind cannot possibly, with any amount of effort, conceive of a God that is beyond "time", beyond the beginning! The highest God that the human mind and intellect can conceive of is one who was there after the beginning. And I am now speaking of a dimension of consciousness that lies beyond time itself! Even when no time existed, we, as conscious beings existed! The capacity of consciousness, the ability to be aware, was and will remain when all time ends! And those rarest of practitioners of the art of meditation, those who have reached this fourth level of pure spiritual consciousness, have described it as being so luminous and so bright, that the light coming from our solar sun would be like the light of a match in comparison!

Even if you put ten (10) or twelve (12) suns of this solar system together, it would not equal the brilliance of a single soul! Such is the lustre of the human soul! And yet, at this pure spiritual level of consciousness, this immensity of light coming from the human soul looks natural! It seems to be just natural that each of our own conscious selves should have so much light. All of this light has been cloaked and covered by these gross bodies. The physical body, the astral body, the mental body... these covers do not let the light shine through. This light is the light of our own consciousness. But it has been covered by so many masks that we cannot see this light at the physical level of consciousness. But, when we are able to raise the level of consciousness to the fourth level, to the level of pure soul, we are able to experience our own light, as well as the light of all other souls! The most interesting thing is, that as we rise higher in the levels of consciousness, not only do we experience higher wakefulness, but we also experience ourselves over a much larger span of creation! We experience a widening of awareness and a much greater intensity of aesthetic beauty. Everything becomes perfect! Once this state of consciousness has been attained, your life becomes a melody of tremendous harmony, a festival... a celebration! All doubts, all problems, all suffering and misery simply get dissolved! You soar for the first time, and life becomes a great symphony of joy, love and happiness! At the pure spiritual level of human consciousness we are able, for the first time, to know who and what we are.

At this soul level of consciousness, the Socratic challenge to "know thyself" is accomplished! And, at last, we have been able to free our consciousness from all the covers which were coming in the way of attaining self-knowledge. There were the mind, the senses, the physical body, dreams and so on, blocking our "self-awareness". Having transcended the lower levels of consciousness, we are able, at last, to experience our "real self"....the "me" that we had been mistakenly identifying with the covers upon our consciousness. For the first time, one can say... "I KNOW WHO I AM".

Below this level of soul consciousness, one does not know who he is! At the physical level, the body is merely a coat being worn over consciousness. At the astral level, the sensory system of perception through which we experience the world, are merely the "windows" through which our consciousness looks out. The mind is just a house; a framework in which consciousness sits. But at the spiritual level of consciousness, we are able to experience the real self...to experience "pure" consciousness! It is the highest flight of consciousness that one can imagine! Yet I must say to you that this is still not the highest level of human consciousness!

The pure spiritual level of consciousness looks so beautiful, so high and so complete that there doesn't seem to be anything beyond it, and when we try mentally—even intuitively, or by any known process of acquiring knowledge—to think of consciousness beyond this level .... we fail. All known methods of knowing, including intellect and intuition, will lead to the conclusion that the spiritual level is the highest level of human consciousness. Yet, there are some practitioners of the art of meditation, who tell us that this is still not the highest level of consciousness! What, then, is restricting consciousness at the level of pure spiritual consciousness?

What is the final cover which is still being worn by human consciousness? The final cover that is restricting consciousness at this fourth level is that of "individuation". Individuation restricts and limits our consciousness to being only one consciousness among many. At the fifth level of consciousness, at what is called "TOTAL" consciousness, we discover that the entire scope of conscious experience is being had by only one experiencer. You discover that there is only one conscious being .... your OWN self! You transcend the experience of individuality .... of EGO! At this fifth level of consciousness, you come to realize your totality. Individuation itself was a cover. It reduced

33

your consciousness to singularity and individuality. Therefore, it was a lower level of consciousness. The fifth level
of consciousness is the highest level of human consciousness.
Not merely the highest, but the level of total and supreme
conscious experience!

At this level of consciousness, the barrier of individuation
is removed and totality of your own consciousness is experienced unfettered by anything which inhibits its freedom. At
this level of total consciousness, total freedom, total experience,
total awareness and the totality of all possible conscious
experiences are included. There is absolutely nothing that is
lacking at this region of conscious experience. From here,
consciousness has degressed, by successive processes of
sleep-like experiences, to this physical level of consciousness
in which we are having all our experiences. It is the furthest
leap from reality that human consciousness can make. Everything at this physical level of consciousness is dream-like,
illusory .... it is "maya"—the stuff of which dreams are
made. We are born in this maya .... we live in it .... we
think in it .... we even dream in it. We are philosophers in
it .... we are scientists, teachers, doctors and so on. Stretch
your ideas as far as you can, take them higher and higher,
call them infinite or by any name you please—still, you will
remain in maya. It cannot be otherwise! The whole of
human knowledge and human experience at this level is an
illusion, a dream.... maya. Everything that is bound by
the laws of time, space and causation is within maya!

I have tried to explain, to the best of my ability, what
the levels of human consciousness beyond the physical level
would look like. I could not say much beyond the causal
level of consciousness, because the time, space-causation
continuum ends there. Beyond it, there is no time, no space,
no causality. It is like a seed, which flowers when placed in

the time-space continuum. Just as when you take a tiny seed
and sow it, you do not see the big tree contained in it. Yet,
the entire tree is contained in that little seed! It seems a
little funny! But, when we allow time to release the poten-
tiality locked up in that seed, the tree is revealed!

In the same way, when the seed of total consciousness is
placed into the time-space-causation framework, the entire,
infinite, conscious experience of all of the creation is mani-
fested! Everything that has happened, can happen or will
happen, is contained in this level of total consciousness. The
entire experience of billions and billions of years, as well as
all timeless experiences, are included in this level of consciousness. No wonder, then, that when asked to describe this state
of consciousness, the only reply from those who have experienced it has been . . . . wonder, wonder! Nothing more about
it can be said! With this basic understanding about the
levels of human consciousness fully grasped, we are now in
a position to explore some of the "deeper" aspects of consciousness.

This whole world exists because we are conscious.
Consciousness is the "creator" of everything that we are
experiencing at any of the levels of human consciousness.
This "total" consciousness within us is, indeed, the creator of
everything that exists. The world of creation, the world
which exists around us, exists only to the extent to which
we are conscious of it! If consciousness is lost or suspended,
the whole experience of this world is lost. There would be
nothing left to sustain any experience of it. There is no
possibility of the world existing without human consciousness
existing along with it. Without human consciousness being
present, how will there be any experience of such a world?
Who will experience its existence?

The entire creation has come into being from within, not outside. Therefore, it is human consciousness; the capacity to be aware, which sustains our experiences of this and all other possible worlds. This capacity to be aware (consciousness) does not ever change! Experiences change, but the "experiencer", the human consciousness, never undergoes any change. It never has, and never will! All changes are "illusions" created by the human mind. It is the human mind which converts our capacity to have conscious experiences into the additional capacity to have experiences in time, thereby introducing the sensation of "change". When total conscious experience descends to the level of universal mind, it is divided into time—into beginnings, middles and ends, into todays and tomorrows, into days and nights, and so on. But this is only a DIVISION of conscious experience. Consciousness itself has not been divided!

These changes and motions in conscious experience are caused when consciousness functions through the time-space and causation framework. What are these things, time-space and causation? Are they something real, or just an idea? The German philosopher, Immanuel Kant, offers an explanation which is consistent with what Eastern philosophers have been saying for thousands of years. He states that there is no such thing as time, space and causation. They are simply categories of the mind! THEY ARE THE MIND! Mind is consciousness when it functions through the time-space-causation framework. The framework IS the mind! When consciousness is pumped into experience and picks up a beginning, a middle and an end, this is called mind. It becomes what we call a "mental" experience.

This mind, then, is the cause of all the changes we experience. We are still capable of knowing our own consciousness at this level, but it will be in terms of changes.

36

From the level of the mind, our conscious experience is then projected into the sensory system, and gets even further divided into sense perceptions. Each sense, in turn, then picks up a piece or a part of our conscious experience. Even then, consciousness, per se, has not been broken up into these functional divisions of the senses.

Finally, on top of all this, the gross physical body is added. When conscious experience functions through the organs of perception in the physical body, it limits our experience to grossness, completely cutting us off from the original experience of "pure" total consciousness! But, even at this lowest level of conscious experience, human consciousness itself, the "experiencer" of all conscious experience, remains absolutely the same! Consciousness, which uses a soul, a mind, the senses and the gross physical body, remains unchanged and unaltered, at every level of human consciousness! It persists at all times and beyond all time! Human consciousness is never born and, therefore, never dies, never disappears.

The question naturally arises whether the self, whether total consciousness, which takes many other forms, itself has a form? When self-realization, when total consciousness is achieved, in what form will we experience it? Does total consciousness, from where all conscious experiences flow, have a form? Yes! It has a very subtle form, the form of a resonance, a vibration ... the form of a SOUND! This "sound" is emanating from the self, from the "atman", from the soul of man! When we raise the level of our consciousness to that of total consciousness, we discover that this sound is actually coming from the total self! This sound originating from the total self, the ultimate creator of our conscious experience, manifests itself as an individuated soul! This sound is the form of our own consciousness. It sounds strange, but it is the truth. If I were to tell you that it is because we can "listen" to the "sound" of our own consciousness that we are able to have any experience, you will be very surprised. But it is the truth! All our perceptions: seeing, tasting, touching, and so on, are possible because we "listen" to this sound of our own consciousness. All these perceptions give us an experience because we can "listen".

When you see a thing with your eyes, how do you "know" what you are seeing? After seeing it, very quickly, almost simultaneously, your mind says to you, that's a flower or that's a house. When it says this, and you LISTEN to your own thoughts about what you are seeing, you then "know" what it is that you are looking at! These eyes cannot pick up any "meaningful" experience, unless the mind "comments" on what is being experienced! You have to listen to the "thoughts" accompanying sense perceptions, in order to have a conscious experience of the objects perceived.

You cannot hear without listening; you cannot see; you cannot taste; you cannot touch or smell without listening to the thoughts—to the "sound" accompanying these experiences in your consciousness. You can have no perception without listening! Therefore, listening or "surat", the power to listen, is the basic and most fundamental faculty in human consciousness. At the highest level of consciousness, it is found that "nirat", the power to see, is simply an extension of surat, the power to hear! Therefore, the capacity to be heard is the chief characteristic of human consciousness. It is no wonder that God . . . the ultimate Creator . . . total consciousness, has been described as a "SOUND"! As that which can be heard! As that which can be listened to! No wonder that St. John's Gospel says that, "in the beginning was the "WORD" and the word WAS GOD!" No wonder that the Hindus believe that "OM", the first word of the Vedas, was the creator of the universe! No wonder that "Shabd", the "SOUND", has been described as the creator of this universe! No wonder the Greeks say that the "LOGOS"—the word—is the creator! That the Koran says that "KALMA"—the word or sound—is the creator! It is no small wonder why every major religion in the world, without exception, has used the same term, in its own language, to describe the creator as the word . . . the sound . . . that which can be heard! Whether it is Islam, Christianity, Judaism, Buddhism, Hinduism or any other religion, you will find that it is the sound, the WORD which has created this entire universe! If there was a beginning, the only thing that was there was the "WORD". It's remarkable! And whatever exists is a manifestation of this "current" of sound emanating from our total consciousness! One who becomes conscious of the highest manifestation of the sound, becomes one with the ultimate creator; becomes one with . . . the LORD!

Therefore, the whole discovery of what is the "real" self, is the progressive discovery of the nature of our own consciousness, which we call the soul. The soul is known when we can experience our own consciousness, without the covers of the mind, the sensory perceptions and the gross physical body. Total self is realized when we are able to remove the final cover of individuation. When all these things have been done, you are able to say that you "know thyself". That you are total consciousness, that, indeed, you are . . . God!

V

THE MIND IS NOT ALL

WE are all trying to solve the problems that face us intellectually (with the mind). We are somehow convinced that the intellect is the best source—the best instrument in human awareness for the acquisition of knowledge; that it has the capacity to solve all of our problems. This belief, however, is erroneous. The problems of life cannot be solved by the thinking process alone. On the contrary, it is because of too much thinking, too much intellectualizing, that we are not able to find solutions to our problems. It has led only to the creation of more problems!

Whenever you bring the intellect in, it immediately dissects and analyzes the problem. Where there is only one problem the intellect will divide it into bits and pieces—into so many other problems. When you divide the reality of the situation, you falsify it, and, consequently you go on struggling your whole life trying to solve these additional problems created by the intellect. You simply become confused; totally confused. Intellect, and the excessive use of it, always leads to more confusion—not clarity and certainty. Awareness and intelligence simply become clouded; clouded with doubts created by the excessive use of intellect. With the intellect, no problem can be made clear. Your awareness will become more unclear! But if you could somehow leave the intellect aside, if you could suddenly transcend the mind and its mental processes, clarity and certainty will immediately flow into your awareness—things will automatically become clear! You will simply "know" the answers to all your problems . . . intuitively! But the moment you allow your mind to enter into the problem, then uncertainty, confusion and frustration are experienced. There is no such thing as a "clear" mind; never has been and never will be. It is not the nature of the mind to be so. Mind means division of experience. When you understand the structure of the human mind and intellect, this will then become clear to you.

What is intellect? It is the power in human awareness to break experience apart, into pieces; the power to analyze; the power to see parts of the whole. This characteristic of the intellect to analyze through reasoning, by breaking things into parts and pieces, is what is responsible for the creation of all our feelings of doubt, uncertainty and the experience of all our fears. This may seem to be a strange and startling statement to many. We have always thought that the intellectual process contributes to the clarity and certainty of our conclusions about a thing, especially in Western countries. But, in fact, it leads only to the growth of anxiety, doubt and frustration. It does not contribute to the solving of any of the problems we are faced with in life. Yet, we do not give any attention to other faculties in human consciousness with which we could solve all the problems we are confronted with, i.e., the faculty of human intuition.

The capacity in human consciousness to pick up knowledge through the intuitive process has been dismissed as something which is simply an ephemeral hunch! Something which occurs only once in a while, and then too by accident. There is no educational institution, to the best of my knowledge anywhere in the world, which scientifically and syste-

41

matically trains and develops the individual's ability to pick up knowledge through the use of the intuitive process. It is my opinion that if a person is trained in the use of his intuitive faculty, just as he has been trained in the use of logic and the intellect, he could better understand and meet the problems that he will encounter throughout the course of his life. In order fully to appreciate the value of intuition, and the contribution it alone is capable of making to the scope of human knowledge, I must define what is meant, in terms of the processes in consciousness, by the words reason and intuition. They have been used so loosely and with so many different definitions that you can easily become very confused. For an exact understanding of this subject, an exact grasp of such terminology will be necessary. Understanding the meaning of these words, as I will be using them, will enable you at once to understand exactly what is being explained. It will facilitate the transfer of a great deal of knowledge concerning the proper roles of reason and intuition in the quest for knowledge.

Reasoning is the capacity of the human mind, through the use of words organized in various combinations, to draw a logical inference about the experience with which they are associated. In the process of reasoning, there must always be some premise, some kind of empirical data which is already known, which reason can then use to reach a particular conclusion. The steps that are undergone in connecting the data given to the conclusion reached, are called the steps of logic. Logic, inductive and deductive, is continuously being used by each of us in order to draw inferences and reach certain conclusions about our individual experiences and problems. This process is what is called reasoning. This particular mode or function performed by the human mind has been commonly considered to be the most accurate process available in human awareness for the acquisition of knowledge. In fact, we imagine that the mind can do nothing else except reason. However, this is not the case. There are three parts and functions being performed by the human mind. I must add, in passing, that this classification is being made only for the purpose of understanding the mental process being performed by the mind. Please, do not take them too seriously. Mind is not something material, and, therefore, can have no parts. I am just using this kind of model for the sake of simplifying the analysis of the mental processes generated by the mind in human consciousness. What, then, are these three parts and functions of the human mind?

The lowest part and function of the mind is called sensing. The sensing part of the mind picks up the elements of sense perceptions coming through the physical body and gives them meaning. It does nothing else but absorb whatever is being picked up through the physical sensory system, i.e., through our eyes, ears, nose and so on. Please remember that the frames of experience which are coming through the physical senses, in themselves, have no meaning to us unless the mind interprets them! It is a very strange thing to notice, but if you are merely shown images of what the eyes see, or the few sounds that the ears hear, and so on, it would make no sense to you at all! It is the lowest part and function of the mind, which receives these elements of perception, puts them together and adds meaning to them. The cognition of sense perceptions constitutes the function of the lowest part of the human mind called sensing. Above this sensing part of the mind is the intellect.

Intellect is that part of the human mind which does reasoning and thinking, which makes inferences through the use of logic. This area of the mind is functioning 24 hours a day . . . from birth until death! This part of the mind is functioning every minute that we are alive, whether awake or asleep. We have already made a detailed examination of the excessive use of the intellect, and almost all of our activities in life are being guided by the knowledge generated by this part of the human mind. Above this part of the mind is the third and highest part. This upper part is called the "creative" part of the mind.

The creative part of the human mind rearranges the elements of sense perceptions, including the processes of reasoning that accompany them, and creates a new pattern of experience. This experience is then considered to be new and different. However, nothing new has really been created, except the pattern. What this part of the mind creates is simply a new pattern and design, and not the contents of the pattern. The design is new, but the elements in it always remain the same. It is this higher part of the human mind which performs the function of "creative thinking" that manifests itself in the form of art, music, poetry, etc. These, then, are the three broad functions of the human mind—sensing, reasoning and creativity. However, there is one serious flaw in each of these functions of the human mind, which makes it inadequate as a sole means of acquiring knowledge. All three of these mental processes are confined to a framework of time and space and must obey the laws of causation . . . the laws of cause and effect.

You cannot have sensing; you cannot have any experience of an event unless it is placed in time and space! You cannot reason, use logic or creativity without causality. The causal direction of the event must be known. Every event which occurs in the mental processes of the human mind is confined to the limitation of this framework of time-space-causation! This particular feature of the operation of the human mind has prompted many philosophers, both in the East and West, to suggest that there is, in fact, no such thing as the mind per se; that when consciousness operates within this time-space-causality framework, it is called mind! Mind, they claim, is merely a term which connotes the behaviour of human consciousness as it operates in the time-space-casuality continuum. In order fully to appreciate the significance of what is indicated by this revelation, I will briefly recapitulate the structure of human awareness.

Human awareness, the capacity to be aware, consists of five broad levels. The lowest level is what we might call the physical level of awareness. This level of awareness arises from the identification we make with the physical body. We are continually identifying ourselves with this physical body . . . with that which cannot be me! What is mine, cannot be me! By virtue of understanding this simple statement alone, when I say this is my body—then my body cannot be me! This is my body, I wear it, I possess and use it, but it cannot be me. It is the same as when I say these are my eyes, my ears, my arms, my feet and so on. It does not mean that I am these things. This mistaken identification of the self, as being this physical body we are wearing, constitutes the lowest level of human awareness.

Our relationship with the entire world is based on the identification with the physical body at this lowest level of human awareness, i.e., father, mother, son, daughter, brother, sister, boss, friend, etc. All these relationships with the world we are experiencing are based on this identification with the physical body. When the mystics and philosophers speak about the lowest level of human awareness, they are referring to the awareness arising when consciousness is restricted to the physical body. Therefore, this body-awareness, which we consider so important, is in fact the lowest level of human awareness. Next, above this, would be the awareness which arises when consciousness operates via the sensory system alone, unidentified with the physical body.

45

But even when consciousness functions purely through the use of the sensory system, this awareness has also been mistakenly attributed to the physical body and its senses. For example, we feel that we are able to see only because we have these physical eyes, when in fact, even when these physical eyes are closed, we are still able to "see". We are able to visualize our friends, our homes, children and so on! Of course, you can say these things are not really there—that they are just being imagined—but I am not talking about whether they are really there or not. I am talking about the capacity to "see". Vision—the capacity to see; to have sight. This capacity is not restricted to the physical eyes! It is not based on or does not arise from the physical eyes, yet we are always saying that we are able to see only when we use these physical eyes! The physical eyes can only see physical things but we have the capacity to see things that are not physical. Can the physical eyes see our dreams or an abstract idea? The "seeing" is the same. Only, that which is seen is different. The same is the case with hearing. We feel we can only hear through the use of the physical ears, when, in fact, we are hearing without the physical ears all the time—twenty-four hours a day! We are listening to our own thoughts. How else can we know what we are thinking? These physical ears do not hear these thoughts. Yet, is the experience and quality of this hearing any different? No!

Therefore, the capacity to listen or to hear is independent of the physical ears. The case is exactly the same with each of the other sense perceptions. They all exist and function, per se, on their own and independent of the physical body. The assumption that sensory perceptions are confined to the use of their respective organs in the physical body is an entirely mistaken notion—a myth! In fact, if we could somehow retain consciousness, while eliminating our awareness of the physical body, we would still have experiences consisting of all of the sensory perceptions! When we are able to develop the capacity to experience awareness through the sensory system, without the use of, or dependence on, the organs of the senses located in the physical body, this would constitute the second level of human awareness which is sometimes referred to as the "astral" level of awareness. Above this is the mental level or "causal" level of human awareness.

At the causal level of awareness, it is discovered that it is not necessary to divide experience into the different sensory perceptions! At the two lower levels of awareness, there was the illusion that unless experience is picked up through the physical senses or is perceived independently with the astral awareness, there could be no experience of the world. But, at this third level of awareness, we discover that the mind has the capacity to pick up experience without having to divide it into multiple sensory perceptions! For instance, consider the experience of abstract ideas. When we speak about various abstract concepts, we understand and know them without use of the sensory system of perceptions—the experience is direct. It is not seen, heard, touched, and so on. It is an experience that does not require the use of the senses. It is experienced directly through the mind. If you examine this phenomenon a little closer, you will find that all of our experiences can be directly grasped by the human mind. They need not be divided into sense perceptions.

We have become accustomed to using only the sensory system in order to experience the world. Therefore, we make the erroneous assumption that it is the sensory system which enables us to have the experience of the world around us. A much more complete experience of the world becomes available to human consciousness when we are able to function at this third level of awareness. The fourth stage in the level of human awareness is when even the mind is not needed in order to have experience! It is the level of intuition and we will explore it, in detail, in the next chapter.

Finally, there is the fifth and the highest level of awareness. It is discovered at this level of awareness that all the restrictions on human consciousness have been removed except one—the limitation of individuation. Even when you are able to experience the world independent of the physical body, the sensory system and the mind itself, this intuitive experience is still an individual experience. This individuation itself becomes a restriction and limitation on human consciousness. At this fifth and the highest level of awareness, the discovery is made that the entire scope of human experience is being experienced by only one experiencer! That there is only one conscious being . . . the self! You transcend the experience of multiplicity, of individuality, of the illusion of the many! At this level of awareness, you discover the totality of consciousness. Then there is no such thing as individuality.

I have given this very brief description of each of these levels of human awareness to remind you of man's capacity to have awareness at much higher levels containing much higher knowledge and to show you that the intellect, over which we take so much pride and so many pains, is not the only instrument and source for the acquisition of knowledge. Intellect belongs to the second part of the third level of human awareness (the level of the mind); the level at which human consciousness operates within the time-space-causality framework.

———

VI

THE ROLE OF INTUITION

HAVING understood the structure and anatomy of the levels of human awareness, we will now return to our examination of the mind, intuition and the details of the fourth level of consciousness—the level of awareness from where the intuitive process in human awareness arises. From this fourth level of human awareness, intuition flows and we are able to transcend the limitations of time, space and causation. We are able to pick up knowledge in experience, without any use of the mental processes, without sensing, reasoning or creative thinking! All "knowing" at this level of awareness takes place through the faculty in human consciousness which is called the "human soul".

The entire quantity of awareness possessed by man is contained and distributed by the soul to the lower dimensions of consciousness; it is the original source in you of all life . . . of all your movements and activities. The human soul is the force which impels you to be alive; the force which sustains your being! It is the source of all human awareness, and yet there are millions of people who do not believe in the existence of the human soul! Many people consider themselves very intellectual and rational; for them everything requires proof! They say that there is no scientific proof of the existence of the soul—that it is not something substantial or that if it exists at all, it is simply a by-product of the processes going on in the physical brain. It does not exist independent of the body and the brain; it merely comes into being . . . it does not PRECEDE being! There is no soul. Where, they insist, is the proof of its existence? To these people, I say, how can you doubt the existence of this "doubter" (the one who is doing the doubting)? Eyes and ears do not doubt. What is doing this?

You cannot doubt the existence of your own consciousness! No proof is required. Its existence does not depend on logic and science . . . it is existential. You cannot say, "I don't know whether I exist or don't exist", this is absurd! How can you say "I don't believe that I exist"? There is no way to deny that you, the soul, pure consciousness without body, without senses and the mind . . . exist! Everything else can be doubted.

One of the greatest Western philosophers, Descartes, used doubt as a method to reach this same conclusion. He started his search for truth with doubt . . . very penetrating doubt. He was the consummate philosopher! He understood that unless there is a known basic fact, which cannot be doubted, he could not construct a philosophical system; there would be no foundation to build upon. If everything could be doubted or had to be proved with tricks—with words— then the whole thing would be just logic. It would have no practical or actual significance. Something deep down must be indubitable, which does not need any proof. Descartes, starting from this point, goes on examining one thing after another until, ultimately, he comes to the soul . . . to his own indubitable existence! The self, the soul, is indubitable because it is SELF-EVIDENT! No proof is needed; no argument and no logic is required . . . it is self-evident. Descartes realized "cogito, ergo sum"—I think, therefore, that I exist, I am conscious, therefore I exist!

I have said so much because in the West we find very few people who will acknowledge the existence of the human soul. Even when they do acknowledge its existence, there are even fewer who make a distinction between the soul and the mind. The mind is abstract; thinking is abstract. The mind, without the aid of the soul, cannot experience reality. It cannot touch, it cannot see, it cannot hear or have any experience independent of the consciousness it derives from the human soul; it cannot experience reality. It can only think and, through thinking, contemplate upon the experiences being picked up by the human soul. It is an epiphenomenon.

The point which must be understood, in order to enjoy the distinction between the mind and the soul, is that the mind does not possess its own consciousness! It is not as if there are two beings within us, one mental and the other non-mental. There is only one conscious being; consciousness is being derived only from the human soul. The mind has no consciousness of its own! It is simply a device used by the soul in order to have a certain species of conscious experience. The mind and the mental processes it performs is being sustained by consciousness arising from the human soul; but because consciousness is constantly flowing through the mind, we get identified with it. We feel that we, as conscious beings, are the mind! This false identification with the mind is called ego. It is this ego which gives rise to our assumption that the mind is the source of human consciousness, and, therefore, is the same thing as the soul. When, in fact, the difference between them is so immense, in terms of the quality of experience arising from each, that there is not even an overlap between the two!

The human mind, as stated earlier, functions only in time, space and causation, whereas the soul functions only OUTSIDE of time, space and causation! There is nothing common between the two! The soul of every human being has the capacity to have conscious experiences which do not suffer from the limitations of time, space and causality. This must be clearly understood. Soul is the capacity in human consciousness to use intuition. Suddenly, a flash of knowledge comes to us, we just "know" something! When did we seek it; when did this "knowing" happen? Where? How? These questoins have no answers because there is no time, space or causality accompanying the function of the intuitive process in human consciousness. Very often, this sudden flash of knowledge is rejected by us because it is sometimes quite inconsistent with what the mind has been thinking. The reasoning process says that we should do this or that and suddenly an intuitive flash comes, which is very often inconsistent with logic and inconsistent with the conclusion reached through the mind. Yet, this non-mental "knowing" is always right! Intuition has never been wrong. The human soul, the capacity in consciousness to experience knowledge which lies beyond time, space and causation, also gives man the capacity to have another type of intuitive experience—the experience of LOVE; the capacity of complete identification with another human being.

Whenever you experience love for somebody it is a sudden, timeless, causeless, and spaceless experience! This great experience of love, which makes us lose our own identity and transfers all our attention to the beloved, does not occur in time, or space; nor does it follow the laws of causality! It does not result from any of the mental processes of the mind. One minute it is not there, and the next—it has totally consumed us. Afterwards, the mind can think about it, but this thinking and contemplation becomes a part of the mental process. Therefore, this "thinking" about love will take place in time, space and causality. It very often happens that the mind, by thinking so much about what is happening during this experience of love, destroys the experience altogether!

52

When you fall in love, the mind says, "Why have you fallen in love with this person?" You try to find some reason for it. Perhaps because she is beautiful, maybe it's her personality which attracts you, and so on. However, this is not the case. These things are beautiful because you HAVE fallen in love! This is what you do not understand! That is why you are also perplexed about other people's "love". You think the person is crazy; that he has gone mad! How could he or she love this kind of a person! It does not make sense! Love never makes sense because love does not come from the mind and its mental process; it is not a logical phenomenon! That is why we call it "falling"—you fall from the pinnacle of reasoning. You "FALL" in love! You lose your sense of reason; you go mad! Love is a sort of madness because it is not logical at all. The experience of love is of such a nature that it cannot be explained.

But without love, man is simply a corpse. Minus love, life is nothing but misery. Plus love, life is bliss. Minus love, you are an empty void—a black hole. Minus love, you are only pretending to be alive, but you cannot really live! How can there be life minus love? LOVE IS LIFE! With the experience of love, your life starts soaring for the first time—you have wings. Minus love, you are just crawling on tiny speck of mud, floating aimlessly amidst the appalling immensity of the physical universe! The significance of human existence is justifiable only if love is being experienced! The human soul, the capacity in human consciousness to experience love, as well as higher knowledge, also enables man to have another type of intuitive experience—BEAUTY. The experience of aesthetics.

Whenever we experience the beauty of a thing, the experience is identical with the experience of love and intuition. It does not subject itself to any of the laws of causality, time and space. When you look at a beautiful landscape or a beautiful painting, you experience the beauty of these things intuitively! If you analyze the whole landscape, part by part, you will not be able to find any beauty! The beauty is coming from the totality of the experience. It is a synthesis of all the parts of its composition, and this experience of the oneness is called beauty, and is being experienced by the soul of man! When you have the experience of beauty, it comes in a sudden flash of intuition. It is experienced when the mind has become completely silent. When you are not aware of the stream of thoughts flowing in it .... when verbalization ceases .... when the intellect has shut down ... when you are in a state of "no-mindness" .... this is when beauty is experienced! When the mind returns, when intellect again takes possession of you, when you contemplate on what you are experiencing, the experience of beauty is lost.

These experiences of beauty, love and intuitive knowledge do not arise from any of the mental processes of the human mind, whatsoever! They are arising from the fourth level of higher awareness .... from the soul of man. It is an awareness which arises from a much deeper part of human consciousness which is beyond the scope of the intellect and the mind; and yet we do not regard intuition as a different function in human consciousness from that of the mind. We go on thinking that whenever the mind, working very fast, is able to execute the steps of logic rapidly, it is intuition. However, this is not the case. Intuition is something that arises in consciousness separately from the mind. The mind is incapable of the "pure" intuitive process.

There are certain "psychic phenomena" that are called intuitive, but are actually this other kind of "mental" intuition. This is not the kind of intuition of which I have been speaking. Some people can "think" very quickly, can go through

54

the successive stages of logic very fast, but they are still functioning in time. Suddenly, a thought comes to them and they spend a few seconds thinking about it; then they are able to come up with an answer. Most so-called "psychic" people, who are able to do these things, are merely capable of thinking very fast, and so are capable of "mental" intuition. They are capable of reaching certain conclusions very quickly, which would otherwise take a much longer time to be reached via the process of reasoning. Now this particular capacity of fast-paced thinking, of coming up with a quick answer, is not "pure" intuition. Their answer could be wrong or right because they are still using the mind. On the other hand, the pure intuitive flash of knowledge requires no time—not even a few seconds, and its answers are NEVER WRONG! The distinction between the two would be in terms of accuracy and time. In the pure intuitive process, no errors are ever made and no time is taken to know the answer.

Therefore, there is a very basic difference between the intuition which is based on the use of the mind, and that which arises from the soul of man. The intuition of which I am speaking is the capacity of human consciousness to function without the use of the mind. Now, the only question which remains is whether we can use this capacity of consciousness wilfully? Is it possible that we can use the mind up to a point, and then switch over to the use of intuition? Is there any particular technique or training available which can enable us to learn how to use the intuitive process? If there is, then we could avoid the numerous problems which result from the exclusive use of the mind. The reply that has been given by these Eastern philosophers and mystics is .... YES! All this can be done. They have said that there can be systematically arranged programmes to educate man in the use of intuition, just as there are schools which are designed to develop man's skills of reasoning and use of logic!

All of our schools and educational programmes are arranged to build up the individual's power of analysis; the power and capacity to break and divide things into parts. Reasoning and logic then proceed upon these parts in order to reach a conclusion about the whole. Our entire educational system, and all the processes and techniques of teaching, rely upon the use of the analytical faculty .... the intellect.

The result is that whenever anyone comes out of a university, he has simply become a machine—a computer! It is as if he has no soul .... only intellect! And then he creates problems wherever he goes. He will create them because the university has given him only intellect and ego and nothing else. He has neither learned a single bit of humanity; nor one bit of humility. He has not touched a single bit of his soul! He has been stuffed with intellect, and this intellect gives him the feeling that he is very significant and important because he has a lot of so-called "knowledge"! He becomes identified with the intellect, with the mind .... the ego is strengthened, and now he creates every kind of problem that is humanly possible.

He will separate and divide life into politics, economics, and so on, which in turn breed jealousy, ambition, violence, cut-throat competition and constant struggle! We have intellectualized life! We have cut it up into bits and pieces, broken it into parts and are now wondering where the beauty of life has gone. The method of the intellect is to separate and divide. There is no other way in which the intellect can function except by breaking things apart, euphemistically referred to as—analysis, whereas the soul of man functions not by breaking experience apart, but by joining things together by synthesis .... by LOVE! By synthesis we experience the beauty of the whole. When we experience life in its totality, the beauty of life reappears! The intuition, this much greater capacity for experience, which lies hidden in every human being is being destroyed by an excessive use of the intellect. We have not done anything to develop this higher faculty available in human consciousness.

We must use this faculty of intuition, of synthesis, which enables man to experience things as a whole, to experience things totally! We have been trained to see only bits and pieces of a thing, and yet what our inner consciousness really wants to have is the total view—the total knowledge of things. Only the intuitive faculty in human consciousness can provide this. The intuitive process draws upon the totality of experience, which has taken place in consciousness throughout its enire history, and throws up, into our awareness, the answer! Reasoning, on the other hand, picks up only a tiny part of our experience, applies logic, and then reaches its conclusion. It is sometimes right and sometimes wrong. All logic, whether inductive or deductive, proceeds upon a given premise. A premise is merely a part of the experience which becomes the subject of our thoughts and the reasoning process. When we apply deductive logic to a premise, we gain no new knowledge. When we apply inductive logic, we can never be certain about the conclusion. In either case, the situation remains the same—unchanged.

Very often, the data that we proceed upon is itself inadequate. Sometimes we reason out exactly what we would do in a particular situation, and then later we find that what we had decided on was wrong. Not because the logic itself was wrong, but because we didn't know, at the time of our decision, the other additional data which was relevant to the situation! The absence of adequate data leads to wrong results, and this happens whenever we use the process of reasoning to make our decisions. This is one of the biggest flaws and weaknesses of reasoning. It must rely, in most cases, on inadequate data, thereby making it incapable of supplying accurate and total knowledge. The process of reasoning proceeds from a given premise—a part of experience which is always limited. On the other hand, this limitation of data does not occur in the use of intuition.

With the intuitive process, there is no deliberate choosing of a particular set of data or premise. Intuition draws upon the total conscious experience of the human being! (The unconscious experience of the past as well as that which lies within the immediate awareness of the individual.) The intuitive process is based upon the entire scope of the individual's experience and knowledge! Not only of one's self (of one's personal past), but that of the whole history of mankind as well! This may seem hard to believe for those who are hearing it for the first time, but this total knowledge of experience is in fact being transferred from person to person, through the genetic principle. This huge storehouse of knowledge, containing the unconscious memories of the entire experience of human evolution, is accessible through the use of the intuitive process. INTUITION is based on this knowledge of the totality of the human experience. By having access to the entire history of human experience, it is easy for intuition (the soul of man) to arrive at the smallest details of a given situation and determine, with absolute precision, everything connected with it! When man uses the intuitive process in human consciousness, it is not confined only to the knowledge picked up from selected data. Therefore, when intuition has been developed and is properly functioning, it can never go wrong! This is the experience of all those who have trained their intuition. They have found that a properly trained intuition never goes wrong. Whereas, even the best and most highly trained intellect very often reaches wrong conclusions—not because of any flaw in logic or in the reasoning process, but simply because of the inadequacy of the data being used. However, this does not suggest that there can be no deficiency in the reasoning process itself.

A well-known professor of philosophy at Harvard University, Professor Charles Sanders Pierce, has written several very interesting books in which he examines the deficiency inherent in the logic used in the reasoning process. In one of his books, he has dismissed the use of certain types of logic because they are entirely useless when applied to the non-mathematical world. He points out that certain syllogisms, like A equals B and B equals C, therefore A equals C, and so on—are never practical in the real world. In this world, it is never the case that any A equals B.

Therefore, to talk in terms of a theoretical model which has no practical application clearly means that this kind of logic is of no use in this world. The real world of people consists of an entirely different kind of relationship. If A "LOVES" B, and B "LOVES" C.... in the real world we find that it does not logically and necessarily follow that A "LOVES" C! "A" may or may not love "C"! When we use logic of this kind to solve problems in the world of mathematics and physics, there is no possibility of going wrong because these relationships will follow the rules of logic, but when this same logic is applied to man, to a conscious living being, there is every possibility of going wrong! Life does not follow the rules of logic, life has its own hidden laws, and you cannot reduce them to any kind of formula or equation. Therefore, ordinary logic, when applied to people and to real situations in life, FAILS! Syllogisms have no practical value when we consider real situations and circumstances of life; a new set of rules must be introduced. Ordinary logic which insists that if A equals B and B equals C, then A equals C, is unrealistic and cannot be applied to the relationships which exist between human beings. It is completely useless in all matters pertaining to practical life, especially in our personal relationships. Interestingly enough, this Harvard philosopher goes on to formulate an alternative set of equations designed to meet our human needs.

However, the point I simply want to make is that we have been over-emphasizing the use of logic and reasoning to the extent that we have shut out our capacity to use our intuition.... the other faculty of knowing which exists in human consciousness. This faculty of ours has been completely ignored, and we must look at the mehods of developing the intuition and the use of the intuitive process reliably; not accidentally—and at will!

VII

A MATTER OF CONCENTRATION

THE methods and means of developing the intuition are as simple as, if not simpler than, the methods which we are using for the development of the intellect and reasoning process. How do we learn how to use the reasoning process? By the manipulation of "attention" and concentrating it upon the subject or object we wish to understand! When we want a student to understand something, to understand what is written in his book, we tell him to concentrate on what he is reading—to "pay attention" to the book! It is the attention of the student that we want to be concentrated upon the book, and when this is done sufficiently, the student "learns" what is within the book. The same principle applies to the learning of anything. Whatever you wish to know or learn will involve the use of the human attention.

What is attention? Attention is that part of awareness which we use in order to focus our consciousness upon a part of our experience, to have a closer and deeper awareness of that particular thing. When attention is concentrated upon the object or subject we wish to know or understand, the growth of knowledge automatically takes place! Therefore, this same process of concentrating the attention has been used by those who have developed their intuition. Exactly how does the student go about concentrating his attention on the book? What is he actually doing? What he is doing is "shutting" off his experience of all the other things going on in his field of awareness, EXCEPT for the object or subject of the learning process! It is only when the student is singularly aware of the book, when he has "suspended" his awareness of the other things around him, do we say that he is concentrating!

When this state of awareness has been achieved, what is written in the book becomes a part of the child's knowledge and learning. In the same way, we should also be able to concentrate our attention on the intuitive processes going on within human consciousness, by withdrawing it from the mental processes going on in the mind! How do we proceed in doing this? Reflect for a moment on what these mental processes of the mind were that we discussed earlier. They were sensing, reasoning and creativity. So, if we take our attention off these mental processes of the human mind, and focus it on the remaining part of our consciousness, we would, in fact, be training ourselves in the use of intuition. It is through the use of human attention, the capacity to attend or not attend to a particular thing, that we are enabled to learn the art of using the intuitive process of knowing. It is one of the greatest gifts that God could have given to man! But first, our attention has to be trained because we have no attention span at all!

Our attention has become flickering; it has become scattered, moving from this to that and from here to there. Not for a single moment are we fully attentive. Even as you are reading this, you are not paying attention! You read one or two lines, and then your attention goes somewhere else; then it comes back. You read a few more lines and then, again, your attention has gone somewhere else. Only a few lines written here and there have really been read. The rest is your own mental creation! Attention represents a state of awareness with no distracting thoughts interfering; it represents a silent alertness. First, our attention must be developed, and the only way we can develop it is by using it!

If we are able to withdraw our attention from the distracting processes going on in the mind and are able to retain our individual awareness, free of interference, we would quickly become proficient in the art of using the intuitive process. This intuition is flowing within human consciousness all the time! We are continuously receiving intuitive flashes. They are a much more reliable source of knowledge than any mental process in consciousness, and are available to us, if only we are willing to make use of them. Intuition is a far more reliable instrument than intellect. The means and methods of developing intuition are available.

Any individual who wants such knowledge must himself make the initial efforts to find the sources of it and to approach it, taking advantage of the help willing to be given to him. This knowledge cannot be given to people who put in no effort on their own part. We understand this perfectly well in connection with the acquisition of ordinary intellectual knowledge, but in the case of this "higher" knowledge we find it possible to expect something different! Yet, at the same time it is essential that one understands that by one's own independent efforts to attain something in this direction there will be no results. An individual can only attain this knowledge with the help of those who possess it. Fortunately, there are especially designed institutions with a training programme where the knowledge of the use of the intuitive process can be learned—where the art of the use of intuition can be learned from those who have mastered it. The intuitive process cannot be learned by merely thinking about it. It is not a matter of scholarship. Do not make the mistake of thinking that, because I have made it all seem so simple, an individual can teach himself this process by reading a few books.

There are many great books full of information about this subject. Very great masters of this technology have existed. They have written everything that could be expressed in words concerning this subject. You can memorize their teachings, but you will not learn how to use the intuitive process by reading these books! Through the study of books alone, you will simply get lost in thinking and in contemplating the subject. All your knowledge will simply be borrowed and impotent. Your conclusions will have no roots in experience and will simply remain the product of logic and reasoning. Many students who fall into this trap just look up for answers in books. They get the answers, but they do not know the process by which they are found!

The problems are given and the answers to them are also given. They simply memorize the answers and then think they "know". They know the problems and they know the answers, but they never know the process. They never "know" how the answer is achieved.

With the study of books alone you will simply go on thinking and thinking about the answers, whereas the objective of learning the art of using the intuitive process is to be able to "know" the answers without using the thinking process at all! The mind is abstract—thinking is abstract, and when this abstract faculty of the human mind tries to reach the plane of intuition, it can only THINK about it! It can never experience awareness when this thinking goes on all the time! Therefore, there must be a special technique used in order to become temporarily unaware of the mental processes. It is here that there is a need for a very highly trained teacher, who is himself skilled in the art of using the intuitive process without the interference of the mind.

First of all, the teacher, as already said, must himself be a practitioner of the intuitive process and not merely a person of scholarship; not someone who has simply read a lot of books on the subject, but someone who has practised and mastered the art of using the intuitive process. The teacher must be someone who has mastered the technique of shifting the attention from experiencing consciousness through the mind to experiencing consciousness free from the distractions of the mental processes. Only someone like this could transfer to us the knowledge of the intuitive process and the techniques for concentrating our attention upon conscious experiences without the use of reasoning. The teaching method employed would not simply be that of the transfer of scholarship! This you can get from books on the subject. This "special" kind of teacher will be capable of transferring pure understanding!

The transfer of scholarship is not as important as the transfer of understanding. Whenever you meet a really inspired teacher, you feel that what he teaches is very, very clear! You feel that you did not have to use too much reasoning at all! You did not have to bring a certain knowledge of the subject with you! Yet this kind of teacher is capable of transferring understanding and knowledge in a way that is far more effective than by studying mountains of books on the subject. His depth will reach your depth. He will become an invocation; his very being will do something to you. He will touch you deep down. Just as you see the full moon at night, and you suddenly become silent—its depth, its beauty and majesty touch you. Similar is the case with such a teacher, but he touches you deeper than any full moon can touch; deeper than anything in the world can touch you. This feeling flows from the intuitive levels of his awareness; it flows from the innermost core of his being to yours—just by being near such a person, you are changed!

You are enlightened! What is the difference? How is a teacher of this calibre able to transfer understanding and knowledge in a much more effective way than ordinary teachers and books do? The reason is because such "special" teachers are intuitively transferring knowledge to us, and we are intuitively understanding it!

This high level and volume of knowledge and understanding can only be transferred to us by a teacher who himself is an expert and master in the art of using the intuitive process. The technique he will use for developing the intuition will be the same simple process by which we train the intellect. The only problem is that we are afraid to take our attention off the thinking process going on in the mind. We are afraid that it would result in our lack of efficiency in performing our duties and meeting our personal needs. We do not seem to realize that only a very tiny amount of thinking that goes on in our minds is relevant to the situations in our lives. The vast majority of it is simply a mad mechanism of which we have become prisoners! Thinking is just like walking. When you want to walk, you use your legs. But if you go on moving them even while sitting down, people will call you mad! And if some one says to you, "stop this nonsense!", you will say, "If I stop, then when I want to walk, what will I do? If I rest my legs, they will become less efficient. If I stop, then I will lose the capacity to walk, so I have to use them constantly!" This is madness! But this is what we are doing all the time. We have been trained by our teachers to go on thinking about "things" as long and as deeply as we can—so that this will improve our capacity to function. The more we think, the better our lives will be. The less we think, the worse-off we will be. Look at the madness of it all!

This fallacy of unnecessarily using a process, even when not required, is consciously avoided in the training of the

66

intuitive process. The student is not asked to engage the intuitive faculty 24 hours a day. We do not ask him to shut off his awareness of everything going on in the thinking process for all time. We only want him to be able to focus, at will, his attention on the intuitive process in order to pick up knowledge when needed. After having acquired the knowledge, he can expand his awareness to other things. The knowledge picked up during the use of the intuitive process will simply have become a part of his consciousness and will enhance the other experiences going on around him. The intuitive process, therefore, would require only the temporary blocking out of the awareness of the physical senses and the thinking process.

After the desired knowledge has been acquired, he can again use the physical senses and the reasoning process to express and apply this knowledge to his situations and circumstances. The intuitive process in human awareness will remain available to him whenever he feels the need to have complete and certain knowledge—KNOWLEDGE that is never wrong! Therefore, I am not suggesting that you do not use the reasoning process at all, nor that you use intuition 24 hours a day; you need not altogether dismiss the use of logic, reasoning and the intellect.

VIII

INTUITION

IN creating a model or structure for the purpose of analysis, there can be no better instrument than the intellect. I have drawn this picture of the structure of the human mind and the levels of human awareness in such a way that it will appeal to your intellect! The fact that I have divided the mind into functions and awareness into different levels and so on, immediately won the approval of your intellect! If I had not broken the subjects into sections and categories, you would have rejected the whole theory of intuition. All that has been said so far could never have been said without the use of the human intellect. I would have had no capacity to communicate with you! Therefore, up to a certain point, and I stress only to a certain point, intellect is a very useful instrument. But if we feel that we can attain the highest knowledge available through the exclusive use of the intellectual process, we will be making a great mistake! Therefore, what I am suggesting is that, in addition to using intellect and reason, we should also use our capacity to know things intuitively! We should not let intellect get in the way of our use of this higher faculty available in human consciousness. Therefore, the best contribution that intellect can make to the process of acquiring knowledge is to know and observe its limitations! This would be a great contribution and will relieve the individual of a great deal of frustration and anxiety.

There is no other faculty in the entire scope of human consciousness that can perform this service, except the intellect! To understand this is to have a great insight! To realize that any event or experience taking place beyond the limits of the time-space-causality complex is inaccessible to the human intellect! Try to think about what occurs before it begins; that takes place nowhere, which has not been caused by anything, and the intellect will collapse! The moment any experience in consciousness is taken out of the time-space-causality sequence, the intellect cannot comprehend it—no matter how much effort is made! The only problem is that the intellect itself has not been trained to automatically shut itself down. The intellect will not automatically perform this function unless it has been properly trained and sharpened! Therefore, even for the intellect to perform this service, it will need to be developed to a very great extent! So, I am not condemning the use of the intellect, because it must be developed to a point where we can discover its limitations, thereby enabling us to go beyond logic and reasoning into the realms of knowledge that have been "denied the logicians".

This limitation of the intellect keeps us at a level of awareness where we cannot see truth. No truth can ever come out of logic because no experience is derived from thinking. With intellect you can only *think* about the truth, you cannot *experience* the truth. But logic and intellect can be a good servant. When you have attained a certain experience, intellect can help to explain it, logic can help to make it clear .... But that is all. The greatest contribution that intellect can make to the growth of human knowledge is to discover this limitation; to discover that it can never

69

"know" the truth and that it cannot transcend and grasp any experience which lies beyond time, space and causation! Once this is fully understood, the intellect can then be persuaded to step aside and let the higher faculty of consciousness, intuition, function. It is not necessary to destroy the intellect. The human mind, consisting principally of this intellectual process, need not be destroyed. Unfortunately, you will find many people who are interested in developing higher levels of human awareness, who try to destroy their minds, and some of them have SUCCEEDED! There are madhouses full of this kind of people! But look at the blunder that these people are committing. Who is saying that "the mind is terrible"? What, in consciousness, is making this statement? That the mind is our enemy; that the mind is the only obstacle standing in the way of our enlightenment and so on. . . . What is making these claims? "Destroy this mind and you will attain the highest levels of awareness . . . . What is saying all this?" It is the MIND itself which says all these things! They are trying to use the mind to destroy itself! Look at the absurdity of it all! No wonder, then, that they go mad. This IS madness!

It is not necessary to destroy the mind, but it is necessary to understand the nature of the mind . . . . to understand that it has its own limitations. Therefore, you must take the level of the intellect to a point of development where it realizes that it can go this far and no further. Then alone will the intellect step aside and allow us to use the higher faculty of intuition arising from the soul of man. In fact, it has been said that the human mind is the greatest enemy of man, only as long as it has not been fully understood. When the intellect has been properly trained to perform its functions in human awareness, this same mind becomes man's best friend. Therefore, in the spiritual development of man towards the attainment of higher levels of awareness, the human mind has been the greatest obstruction when not understood and trained. When we fully understand its legitimate function, it becomes man's greatest aid in the journey to higher levels of human awareness. The only problem is in training it.

If we deliberately trained the mind, along with training ourselves in the use of the intuitive process, we would greatly add to the scope and accuracy of human knowledge. Today, one of the greatest drawbacks in our society and in our human relationships is that we are beset with doubts. Nothing is certain; no one knows anything for sure—everyone is simply groping in the darkness, and because of this uncertainty and doubt, great fear and scepticism is created in the minds of men. This fear and suspicion breeds hatred and anger. We are constantly victimized by jealousy, frustration, lack of trust and so many other emotional and psychological diseases of the mind. People have become schizophrenic, split, divided. Our entire society is becoming mentally ill! This is due, largely, to the element of doubt which permeates our minds. We are never really sure about the other person, about our wives or our husbands, about our boss or our neighbour, and so on.... we are never sure of what they will do; of what they are thinking, and so on. All our fears, our lack of trust and confidence, and conflict in personalities occur because of this element of doubt which is present in the human mind. This 'doubt' and lack of knowledge is arising from one thing, and one thing only.... the excessive use of the intellect.

The more we reason, the more doubts we create in the mind. The more we think about a problem, the more confused we become. The mind becomes crowded with so much information and so many alternatives that lack of certainty and confusion is bound to occur! It is a very strange thing

71

to notice. The intellectual process upon which we rely so much, upon which we bestow such acclaim—this process of reasoning and use of logic leads only to more confusion and uncertainty! It generates so many possibilities that we become totally confused. We are, then, not able to decide what to do and, therefore, can do nothing but suffer! The excessive use of the intellect, especially with regard to our human relations, has led to a lack of faith and trust in each other, lack of love, greater conflict in society and violence in general. It is, therefore, the excessive use of the intellect which is causing all our problems in society as well as in our personal lives.

I am suggesting that, in addition to the use of logic and the intellectual processes, we also use our faculty of intuition. The intuitive process will, in turn, generate total and certain knowledge which will enable us to banish these problems of jealousy, hatred, fear, violence, and so on—first from our personal relationships, and then from society as a whole. The knowledge of the goodness of man will be brought to us through this use of intuition. It will enable us to function from a much higher consciousness .... LOVE! Love is the greatest mystery; the greatest mystery that there can be. It can be lived, but it cannot be intellectually "known". It can be tasted, experienced, but cannot be understood! It is something which goes far beyond logic and reason .... something which surpasses all understanding! Love is the highest possible experience available to human consciousness!

This experience of love is being blocked out because of the excessive use of logic and reasoning. Therefore, world-wide training and development of the intuitive faculty in human consciousness is extremely important and necessary.

We should not banish reason and the use of the intellect altogether, but we should learn to use them properly and only when and where they are required. We should not supplant them into areas of human existence where their efficiency is minimized or altogether inadequate. Intellect and reasoning should not be used in the areas of love, human understanding and togetherness, that is in the realms .... beyond logic and reason. All exercises in the development of awareness lead to the experience of "oneness" and love. This total awareness, which is the experience of oneness, is the highest experience which we can visualize or know, in terms of the growth of human awareness. We have had problems in the development of human awareness, because we have had problems in understanding our own self. When we are able to understand our own self, we are automatically (with no further effort; without any other mechanics) able to develop higher awareness and the experience of love.

The more we use the mind, the more we see the difference between ourselves. Different clothes, different bodies, different races, different languages, different religions .... and so on. The intellect always divides people into different categories—the educated and the uneducated, the religious and the sinner, the moral and the immoral; the pattern is always the same. The intellect goes on dividing people into "differences". Then we claim to belong to one of these "so-called" higher categories; that way, we can pretend to be better than others! All these differences between us are being created by the intellect, by the mind. Intuition, the soul faculty in human consciousness, notices only one thing .... the ONENESS of consciousness. It notices the same consciousness—the same light of consciousness that is shining in all of us! The awareness of this "common" consciousness comes through the deliberate use of our intuition. Therefore, when we talk about the development of awareness to the level of the soul, the spiritual level, we are not merely speaking of some abstract level of consciousness. We are talking of the development of one's intuition in order to see the oneness existing among all human beings. This realization is called love, and it can be experienced—at will—by transcending the intellectual processes going on in the mind.

What happens when we transcend the intellectual process? When we do so, instead of approaching anyone or any situation full of doubts, we approach through love, based on the understanding that he or she IS THE SAME THING THAT I AM. That, in them is operating the same consciousness as in me. My trust will beget his trust; my love will beget his love! We are all basically loving creatures because we are made of love. THIS MUST BE REMEMBERED AS MUCH AS POSSIBLE.

You can try this experiment today. No one needs to change his name, life style and so on. We need love. All that we are inwardly concerned with is .... LOVE! But when we function through the process of reasoning, logic and an excessive use of the intellect, we trigger the "mind" response in other people. When we speak with (through) the intellect, with only the mind, we create doubt in the mind of the other person. Then he or she becomes unsure of our motives; doubts whether we are sincere and whether we really mean what we say, and so on. Our intellect will trigger doubt and fear in the other person's mind! When we act out of the ignorance of the "sameness" of human consciousness, the other person picks up our uncertainty and himself responds with doubt. Then come fear, tension and lack of knowledge of each other, which only lead to further misunderstanding! Just replace this whole phenomenon with the language and act of love and trust. Act and speak from the realization that the "other" person is the same as you are, the same soul, the same consciousness made by the same creator .... we are a part of the same thing!

We are able to solve all of the problems we are having in our human relationships by remembering that consciousness, God and love are in EVERYONE. When this oneness can be remembered all the time, we will have no more problems. Our life will become a melody of tremendous harmony; a festival .... a celebration! All our tensions and anxieties will dissolve; and friction amongst ourselves will disappear. Our life then becomes like music .... a great symphony of joy, love and happiness!

IX

BEYOND PHILOSOPHY

IT is said that philosophy is like a blind man searching on a dark night, in a dark room, for a black cat which is not there! Therefore, if you can find any answers through philosophy, remember that this simply means that your question was silly; that your question really did not have any significance; that it was not a question about "reality", i.e., about that which "IS"! For answers to "real" questions, for solutions to "real" problems you will have to go beyond philosophy! In fact, the more one confines oneself to the study of only "academic philosophy" for arriving at "answers" the more confused one becomes by contradictions. Philosophy is unable directly and satisfactorily to answer the vital questions concerning human existence.

The realization of the necessity for a higher level of knowledge—knowledge which surpasses the levels of knowledge attainable by doing tricks with words, with intellect and clever reasoning—has become more and more apparent to modern man. We have come to realize that, in providing us with solutions relating to the fundamental problems of existence, modern philosophy has become almost as helpless as a little child. Philosophy is drifting farther and farther away from its real purpose and is getting bogged down in futile discussions of artificial questions which do not throw any light on the fundamental problems of life.

Academic philosophers are very good at categorizing things. Their whole effort is to put everything in a particular category—this is this, that is that. If you ask them a question, for which they already have an answer, well enough. But if a question is asked for which they do not have an answer, you are in trouble! Their whole approach to knowledge is mechanical! Academic philosophy is mechanical, and how can anything mechanical help you to become wise? They are no longer in search of the organic unity of life; they are no longer in search of the ultimate principle of life that sustains the existence of the trees, of mountains, of a rose and of each and every one of us! They are no longer in search of that unifying factor, the "Philosophia Perennis!— the highest knowledge.... the truth! As there is only ONE reality as the basis of the universe, there can be only ONE ultimate truth which should be the object of pursuit by anything that goes by the name "philosophy"! It is the knowledge of this truth, which is the goal of all "TRUE" philosophy.

As I understand it, philosophy is the art of knowing. Knowing life, knowing one's self, knowing everything, knowing what "KNOWLEDGE" is and knowing the skills and techniques of the process of knowing! In this sense, philosophy and knowledge become synonymous, but the word "knowledge" has been used in so many different senses that it becomes necessary to clarify what is meant here by "knowledge" and "knowing". There are many other words which are mistakenly considered to have the same meaning as the word knowledge. Some of the other words which we confuse with knowledge are: information, memory, understanding, wisdom and awareness. In fact, each of these words actually represents different functions in human consciousness. We very often consider a "wise" man as simply being a man of knowledge. Or we consider a man who has "good" understanding, as a man of "knowledge". Sometimes, people who are able to pick up and store information in their memory are called knowledgeable simply because they can reproduce this data like a parrot .... like a computer! But, only when you are able to "know" something, in a manner which a computer cannot, will you have earned the right to be called knowledgeable! After all, the basic power for having all types of non-mechanical knowledge, including all nomenclatures of knowledge, is derived from human consciousness.

Unfortunately, the word "consciousness" is used very loosely in modern psychology, and even in ordinary parlance. It is used to refer to the principle of human awareness in a very general way. We use the words "consciousness" and "mind" almost synonymously. This is understandable because the two are so closely intertwined in their expression that we can hardly distinguish between them. Nevertheless, it must be fully understood that there can be no "mind" without consciousness, because mind arises out of consciousness! Therefore, if one is not "conscious", there is no question of one being knowledgeable or having any kind of understanding, wisdom and awareness! It then follows, necessarily, that human consciousness is the prime source of power that sustains all the functions and modifications of the human mind, namely, memory.

Another lower form of knowledge—perhaps the lowest—is "information", which is data gathered through the physical sensory system of perception. Our eyes see and our ears hear; our hands feel, our tongue tastes, our nose smells and so on, thereby enabling us to know what we are perceiving. This knowledge of our perceptive experience is just "information" about the experience. This knowledge is then stored in our memory, from where we can recall it and communicate it to others. In spite of the ability to recall and communicate this knowledge through words, it simply remains information!

Next come the sensory perceptions themselves.... per se. Even without the use of the physical organs of perception, we are able to see, hear, taste, and so on. In short, we are able to create experiences through "imagery". Although the operation of the faculty of imagination is very often based upon use of the information obtained through the physical sensory apparatus, at times it can be original and unrelated to the information gathered in this manner. Knowledge, arising from the sensory system of perception per se, is knowledge of a higher kind than mere information. It is this kind of knowledge which inspires great works of art; or scientific invention; of spiritual revelations; of literary breakthroughs and religious miracles! But, knowledge higher than this is the knowledge arising from that part of the mind which is described as reason and understanding. Please note that the human mind has the capacity to perform three different functions. The first, and the lowest, is "sensing"; when it picks up information via the sensory system of perception. Reasoning, and the use of logic, is the second and a higher function of the mind. It is that part which does what we call "thinking". All "thinking" involves the use of words. These words are nothing more than phonetic symbols having a certain connotation based on our association of ideas with them. Thus, the words that each individual utilizes in his thinking process will have a unique and private meaning. No two individuals can have the same association of ideas with the same set of words. Through the process of recalling to memory and through the process of association of ideas,

79

words are used to create a logical cause and effect relationship in the thinking process. This mental process is continuous and goes on in ordinary consciousness all the time.

This, then, is a brief description of the second function of the human mind, namely, logic and reasoning. Knowledge acquired through this process is commonly considered to be a higher form of knowledge than the knowledge which arises from information gathered through the sensory system of perceptions. Philosophy, as it is currently understood, is entirely based on logic and reason. Logic is the foundation of science, but not the foundation of life! Logic and reasoning are only applicable to dead things, because the basic method of logic is dissection, and the moment you dissect something, you kill it! Academic philosophy simply goes on killing people because it goes on dissecting man and dissecting the human experience into categories and parts! Therefore, if you want to find the meaning of life through the study of academic philosophy, through logic—you will never find it! The very process and method being used will prohibit it! Life is like a flower—a rose. You can dissect it, you can "analyze" its ingredients and chemical composition, but you will then miss the most important thing . . . . its beauty! You will not be able to find any beauty, any life, any fragrance . . . . they will all be gone. There will be a few chemicals, but these chemicals are not the "rose"'; these chemicals were simply the "situation", the "circumstances" in which the rose "appeared"! The "rose" has escaped and disappeared into an invisible world. Philosophizing life is like dissecting a dancer—do you really expect to find "dance" inside him? You will find bones, flesh, blood and so many other things, but you will not find dance! You can cut open the throat of a singer, but you will not find the song! The throat is simply a vehicle, a medium. The song comes from a world beyond science or academic philosophy.... beyond logic and reason!

The third and the highest function of the mind is "creative" thinking. It is called creative although nothing is actually "created" except "new" patterns and designs! The mind simply picks up the various elements of sensory perception, churns them and then rearranges this information into different patterns and designs. This whole process is then called "creativity". However, the mind creates nothing new. The contents gathered through the sensing apparatus remain the same and only a "new" pattern, a different "combination" of the elements of perception, is evolved.

There are, however, certain times when the creative mind does overlap with "higher" awareness, which we will examine a little later. But for the present I will return to examination of "knowledge", and its variant.... wisdom. Wisdom is the growth of your own consciousness! It is intrinsic; it does not come from outside. It explodes within you and then spreads to your outer life! When knowledge dovetails, practically, or near practically, with the exigencies of human experience, it is called "wisdom". It is something which must be obtained by each individual by his own effort from the deepest recesses of his own consciousness! Wisdom, unlike information, cannot be "borrowed" from books, lectures, and so on! The difference, then, between a "wise" man's knowledge and understanding, and the understanding of someone who is not wise, consists in the former's ability to "correctly" apply his knowledge and understanding to the situations and problems of real life! A wise man is one whose understanding is "practical"; applicable to the problems of life, and that enhances the experience of joy, love and happiness! Wisdom results from a very highly developed capacity to "understand", combined with a very deep experience of life. The experience may not be long in years, but it would be significant in terms of its impact upon human consciousness.

Therefore, wisdom is a superior form of knowledge, as it couples understanding with practical living. But higher than wisdom is the fully developed human awareness available through the use of the faculty of intuition! It is direct knowledge of the entire human situation. It solves all the riddles of the mind and, therefore, has often been described as the attainment of "total knowledge" or "total awareness".

When human awareness gets developed to this level, it provides us with total knowledge; knowledge which "surpasses all understanding"! Sometimes this level of knowledge has been called "transcendental knowledge" because it transcends the mental processes of ordinary knowledge. Sometimes this knowledge is also referred to as "mystic" knowledge because it can be acquired by various mystic practices. However, no matter what label we give to this higher knowledge, one thing is clear. It encompasses all other forms of knowledge and gives a meaning and interpretation to them. Therefore, philosophy, in the truest sense of the word, must consist of the art and techniques of securing this total knowledge. And, side by side with the quest for this highest level of knowledge, there has always been the simultaneous quest for higher levels of consciousness.

Any intelligent person, who is capable of serious reflection, who is capable of understanding even the most elementary realities of human existence, cannot help but conclude that there is a great mystery hidden behind the universe as well as behind his own life. And until this mystery is unravelled, life can have no real meaning and man cannot be at peace with himself. However, there are people who do not concern themselves with this mystery and instead get involved in their careers, families, and so on. But the "unconscious" presence of life's unresolved mystery will continue to haunt them and poison whatever little happiness they are able to derive from this life.

We have become so engrossed in our ordinary pursuits and passions that we are hardly aware of the hard facts of life which stare us right in the face! If only we would honestly look at these facts, we would tremble. We would be shaken to the very core of our being by their impact. It requires only a little common sense on our part and a little detachment from our engrossing preoccupations to see how utterly meaningless and dream-like the whole drama, being played on the stage of this world, would be if there was nothing more to life. Should we not try to go deeper into the question of human existence and its problems instead of living our lives thoughtlessly?

The deeper problems of life do not cease to exist simply because they are ignored! They will simply appear in the form of some other problem, more serious and far more dangerous to our peace of mind. When society ignores the needs of man's spiritual nature—the need to know the truth—we are temporarily able to do what we like without any inhibition. But, sooner or later, the problem will reappear, perhaps in the form of a nuclear war with the dreadful possibility of destroying this whole planet!

Thirty-five centuries ago, a great continent, Atlantis, disappeared into the ocean. Atlantis was the most advanced society on earth; civilization had reached its highest peak, and whenever civilization reaches a great scientific peak, there is a great danger involved.... the danger of it falling apart. Humanity is again facing the same danger. Scientific breakthroughs have made man very, very powerful. And when there is too much power, and too little understanding, power has always proved fatal. Atlantis committed suicide! Without higher knowledge, scientific growth is dangerous. The whole world is again in a state of chaos. Society is uprooted and life seems meaningless. Moral values are disappearing and a great darkness of evil surrounds us. Our sense of direction is lost. We simply feel that life is accidental. There seems to be no purpose, no significance; life appears to be just a by-product of chance. It seems as if existence does not care about us. It seems that whatever we are doing is futile, routine and mechanical. Life seems to be pointless. You don't know who you are, where you are.... why you are. You feel like a piece of driftwood with no direction. Where are you going? Why were you even born? For what? These answers you do not know. The question mark is there all over your face, why? The reason is because you have not looked into the deepest core of your being! You have not unravelled the mystery which surrounds your being and very existence, and there can be no real peace in life until and unless the answers to these questions are known!

The answers to all questions lie within ourselves, within our own consciousness. I have taken a long time to make such a simple statement as this THAT ALL ANSWERS LIE WITHIN US. And yet, I am not satisfied that I have said enough! I am not sure if you will really look within your self to find the answers. Even if sometimes the desire to search within arises, you again start searching outside. You may still like to read books or listen to lectures to get the answers. Lectures and books, however good they might be, are still outside! They are not within you! Sometimes you go to this place or that place, but why are you going to these places! Somebody goes to India, somebody to Tibet, and so on, but still the search remains somewhere outside! So, even when the right desire arises, you move in the wrong direction!

If you really want to know who you are, you need not ask anybody else. Nobody can answer this question except you! And even if someone answers, the answer will not be "your" answer! At the most, it will be information, and information is futile because it is not "KNOWING"! Not only will this "information" be of no help to you, it will simply create more confusion in you! Therefore, the correct process is first to "GO WITHIN" and then go to these lectures, holy lands, and so on! These things will then serve as a "witness" to your experience. They will authenticate what you already "know", and you will be able to verify their authenticity. Otherwise, all reading, studying or attending lectures, are going to simply create more and more confusion! How will you be able to interpret their validity? You cannot understand more than you have experienced; you can "understand" only that much which you have known on your own, which you—yourself—have experienced.

Consciousness, which is the creator of all experiences, is inside us.... within our own self, and all answers must come from there. The teacher, the "Guru", the master, is within ourselves, and we have to discover him "within". But we have become so accustomed to searching outside that the master residing within us must come outside! He comes outside to talk to us—not because the "truth" is outside—but because we look nowhere else! He says, "I waited for you for a long time within, but you never turned your attention within! What could I do? I became impatient, that is why I have come outside to talk to you! But I am only the "image" of the teacher. The "real" teacher still remains inside you. My role is to "push" you back to your own self!" Hence, the outer master does not impart mere "information".... he imparts "being"! He does not make you more knowledgeable, he makes you more "aware".... more meditative. He will not just give you theories, hypotheses and "academic philosophy"; he will throw you back to your own self. . . . again and again! Sometimes he has to do this in spite of you! Because you want to cling to some "philosophy"; you want clear-cut, ready-made answers; some kind of dogma or doctrine to believe in! Yet, the master will refuse to give you any dogma or theology. In fact, he will take all these ideas from you and slowly he will leave you totally naked! Then you will see yourself as you are and not as according to some doctrine. All this happens within you and you need not go anywhere else. What, however, is this business of "going" within? Can there be a "methodology" for going within and, if so, what?

X

ENTER THE SAINTS, MYSTICS

THE saints and mystics have presented a concept of man that is not easily accepted by most people in the world. The concept is that man, in essence, consists of "pure" consciousness, which is simply functioning through various "coverings" picked up in its descent down into this physical world. Self-realization can be attained simply by removing, one by one, these various covers. Therefore, let us briefly see what these various covers upon the self are, how we got them and how these saints and mystics say they can be removed. According to the analysis of the mystics, what we call the "self" is the totality of our own consciousness. When this "total consciousness" individualizes (splits into many pieces), we call each of these pieces a "spirit" or a "soul". The Eastern philosophers and mystics have called it the "atman". . . . individuated consciousness. Next comes the functioning of this individuated conscious soul through the first cover, the causal body. The causal body is so called because it "causes" all things to happen! Frequently, it is more simply referred to as the mind. There is no distinction between the two. No experience takes place in time,, space and causation, except through the agency of the causal body. . . . the human mind. Just as there is only one single, total consciousness that we call the self or "soul", similarly, there is but one human mind that has been called the "universal mind".

Just as the single, total consciousness individuates itself into individual souls, in the same way the universal mind also individuates itself and becomes an individual mind and has the experience of interacting with other minds! In the Eastern schools of philosophy, the universal mind has been called the level of "Brahmanda". . . . the creator. All things are created from this level. So, in its descent, the soul picks up the universal mind and, together with it, continues its descent into "creation". So, from this point on, below the level of Brahmanda or the "causal level", the soul travels with a cover of the individuated mind over it. Thereafter, all the functions of human consciousness take place through the agency of the human mind. Next, this consciousness, contained in the mind, is further split into what is called the "sensory system". When we experience an event through this sensory cover, it causes us to regard the singular and direct experience of the mind as a split-up experience consisting of hearing, tasting, seeing, touching, and so on. In fact, the sensory sytems of perception are merely devices in awareness to "expand" an experience by dividing it into parts.

Therefore, this division of the mind into sensory functions constitutes yet another cover upon the soul which is very often called the "astral body". This whole complex is then called the "astral self". This astral self, in turn, picks up yet another cover upon itself—the physical body. Once it has taken on the physical body, the sensory functions, which were supposed to be performed by the astral body, are locked up in the physical body. We then begin to feel that if we want to see something, we must use these eyes, to hear we must use these ears, and so on. Therefore, this final covering upon the soul, the physical body, ultimately creates in us the feeling that we are the physical body! That this world—this physical plane of consciousness—is our home! And that the journey back to our original state of consciousness, the one in which we existed without any of these various covers, is simply the journey from the physical self back to the total self! This, then, is real self-realization! If we accept this analysis of our spiritual plight by the saints as being accurate, the question of how these various covers are to be removed naturally arises. We would like to know if there is any methodology or technique we can use, in order to move from the physical self back to the total self within. The mystics and practitioners of the art of yoga and meditation say, yes! They say that there is a very simple and natural methodology by which we can increase our awareness from that of this physical self to that of total consciousness.

One can conceive of a methodology or technology for achieving something outside, for reaching somewhere outside one's self; but for becoming oneself, we need not go anywhere; we need not reach some place outside; we do not have to "achieve" anything. We have simply to be what we already are! Therefore, why should there be any necessity for a methodology? Why should we need any technology or method to become what we are? All methodologies and technologies should be required for becoming something else.... not for becoming what we are!

The consciousness "within" us is the creator of all that we are experiencing around us, it IS what we are! Everything that we are perceiving in this world around us is being "experienced" by this "consciousness" within. The entire creation has come into being from "within", not outside. Therefore, if one desires to know one's self, one must know the consciousness which resides within the physical body. So, the problem becomes how to go "within" this physical body?

89

This body, in which we find ourselves, is the most beautiful product that the Lord has ever made. There are no heavens and paradises; no higher regions or any other forms as marvellous as this human body, through which we are experiencing creation. In this human body, the LORD HIMSELF resides! The "CREATOR" Himself is sitting inside! .... "The Kingdom of Heaven is within you". This human body itself is the "temple of God"! All other temples in which you are spending so much time and energy; in which you go on searching for the self and God-realization, are but monuments and a tribute to this living temple.... the human body!

We have to enter this temple of God, the only real church, the only mosque, the only true place of worship.... through the "gate" which opens into the temple. This body, or temple, has many gates but there is only one that opens "within", only one which leads us to the "inside" of this body; all others are exits. There are nine "exits" in this body from which our consciousness flows out into the world and generates the human experience. They are: the two eyes, the two ears, the two nostrils, the mouth, the reproductive organ and the rectum. These are the nine portals or nine "doors" through which our consciousness—via attention—goes out of this human body. Please note that "attention" does not come into the body via these doors, it can only go out! Nobody can put "vision" into his eyes, it can only flow OUT of his eyes! Similarly, all the nine doors to this beautiful temple of the human body are capable of only the outward flow.... the "exit" of human consciousness.

We have been roaming outside our abode too long. From the very first time we went out of this body through the flow of attention, we have remained outside! You have only to watch the behaviour of your own thoughts. When this is done, you will see how you have become entangled and trapped outside. Through the senses, you have spread your consciousness very thinly throughout experience; you have made many attachments. We have gone outside ourselves and have made all kinds of strong attachments that we are now unable to break, and we cannot, therefore, come back "within" ourselves. We are spending all our time outside! These nine doors that open outwards into the world are being constantly used by us just to make contact with the objects of our attachments! Therefore, being attached, we remain outside our "own self". When our consciousness remains outside, we become identified with the objects of our attachments and forget who we are.... we lose contact with our "self"; the result is loneliness. Fulfilment of this "inner loneliness" is sought from the company of people outside, but this outside company fails to satisfy this "inner" need of the human being, and, therefore, we continue to be lonely. Even when we are surrounded by hundreds of people, we still remain lonely. Something in us is not being satisfied. There is something absent, something "missing" in our life.... the self is not there.

The world is full of lonely people, and because of their loneliness they do many foolish and stupid things in an attempt to fill this void.... this emptiness inside. Sometimes, a person starts eating too much, just to feel full! Someone else turns to drugs or alcohol to escape his loneliness. This loneliness hurts. It's like a wound and is so painful that one wants to soothe it at any cost. The world is a very lonely place, hence people turn to drugs, sex or any and every kind of conceivable entertainment that will keep them anaesthetized! However, this pain of loneliness persists despite our best efforts to escape its clutches. We try to appease it in many different ways—with cars, with big houses, with money, with all kinds of gadgets and toys but still the pain of loneliness persists!

91

Fig. 1

Name	Location	Presiding Deity	Function
6. Ajna Chakar	Center of the eyes Two Petals	Soul and Mind	Enlivens the body
5. Vishudhi or Kanth Chakar	Throat 16 Petals Dark Blue	Shakti	Minor creative current
4. Anahat or Hirday Chakar	Heart 12 Petals Blue	Shiva	Protection and destruction of physical body
3. Manipurak or Nabhi	Navel 8 Petals Dark Red	Vishnu	To nourish the physical body
2. Svadasthan	Genital 6 Petals Whitish Black	Brahma	To prepare the physical body
1. Muladhar	Rectum 4 Petals Reddish Colour	Ganesh	Elimination of physical matter

These six chakras, called DarJat SiflI by the Mohammedan Saints, are the reflections of the six Chakras of Brahmand. These lower Chakras are presided over by the deities, or powers, whose function is only to look after the physical body.

You can have the biggest house in the world, and still you will remain as lonely in it as you were in your basement apartment! These things are not going to make a bit of difference—ownership of this world itself cannot satisfy your inner loneliness! To satisfy loneliness, you will have to go within! You will have to go through the "tenth" door, which opens into our head.... into the "upper room" of this temple where consciousness resides. How do we enter into this human body through the tenth door, in the head which is above the nine doors below? There are many ways of doing this, two of which I will now briefly describe.

One of the ways of doing this is to reverse the direction of the energy flowing outside, and bring our consciousness back through this energy to the tenth door. Since we cannot use these nine doors to come into the body, we can, however, use "energy centres" sustaining this physical body to gain entrance into the tenth door; the door behind the eyes.... the "eye centre". The physical body has two parts. The first is below the eyes and is called "Pinda". The second is above the eyes corresponding to the frontal part of the brain. This is called "Brahmanda", the seat of Brahm.... the Creator.

There are six energy centres or CHAKRAS which sustain and hold this physical body—Pinda—together. (See Fig. 1). If these centres were not operating, this physical body would instantly disintegrate! The lowest energy centre, the Muladhar, is at the rectum. The energy flowing at this centre holds us to the earth and provides us with the experience of gravity. Through this centre, we are able to determine directions. It is also the centre of evacuation; all the waste material left over in the body processes is eliminated through this centre. In Hindu mythology LORD GANESH, the "guardian" of the temple, resides at this centre. All of these powers are then referred to as the power of LORD GANESH. Once we are able, through the concentration of our attention, to enter into this centre, we rise up to the second energy centre of the Genitals, the Svadhisthan Chakra.... the centre of pleasure. This is also the centre of reproduction where all human life is created. It is the centre where the physical body is prepared and created. Therefore, all "beginning", in terms of the physical life, occurs here. The beginning of all physical experience with the body starts and is created at this centre. Huge whirlpools of "creative energy" flow near this centre. The "Kundalini", a vast coiled "serpent" of energy, lies just behind this chakra. The entire energy of the Kundalini can be released by entering this chakra through the concentration of attention. Rising still further from this centre, by the concentration of attention, we are able to gain access to the next centre—the NABHI CHAKRA—the navel centre. This is the chakra or centre in the middle of the stomach. This is the centre of sustenance, of nourishment and maintenance. LORD VISHNU, the God of sustenance, the "sustainer", resides at this centre. In the trinity of the beginning, the middle and the end, he represents the middle.

That energy, the power at the navel centre, provides us with ability to rise higher, through meditation, to the next higher chakra in the body—the "Heart" centre or Hriday Chakra. It is the primary centre and the one that generates permanent experiences. Out of all the chakras so far described, it is only this chakra that provides us with a permanent experience. It is the abode of Lord Shiva.... the Lord of Death! In the trinity he represents the end. Hence, he is often referred to as the "destroyer". Since all things which have a beginning must also have a middle and an end, Lord Shiva— the power at the Heart centre—is considered to be the all-inclusive deity, containing Lord Brahma and Lord Vishnu within himself. Therefore, the experience of death, which arises from the heart centre, is considered to provide the only permanent experience of which we can be certain. The one thing of which we all can be sure .... is death! We cannot be sure of anything else in this life except this. Yet, we can still rise higher in this ascent through the energy centre via meditation to the next higher chakra, the Kanth Chakra.... the centre at the throat.

At this centre of the throat resides the goddess Shakti, the power to create.... the subsidiary power to create. Just as the "creator" of all the experience we are having in the world is created by the creator sitting within this temple behind the eyes.... in the "Brahmanda region", similarly Shakti is sitting at the throat centre and can also create. All dreams are created from here; all fantasies and imaginations are created here. All ideas and inspirations that we project into experience flow from here. We are able, by concentration of our attention—by meditation—, to enter into this centre and have an experience of this higher power which exists in human awareness. However, we can rise still further in this "ascent" of consciousness, to the centre behind the eyes— the Ajna Chakra. It is the centre where our own self and the mind resides. It is the "tenth" door.... the door that opens into this temple of the human body! By entering through this door, we will at last have come home to ourselves and, for the first time, we will be fulfilled. All loneliness will disappear at last.

The other approach would be to destroy the chakras to release their energy while alive; the suggestion is to "die while living".

XI

THE 'THIRD EYE'

B EFORE making a further analysis of this other methodology given by the mystics, let us briefly familiarize ourselves with some of the problems inherent in the process of going within the body via the use of "attention". Immediately, we are confronted with the problem of how to "lose" awareness of this physical body, which is necessary in order to have the experience of what we are without it. Do we have to die? Does this physical body have to be destroyed to enable us to reach our inner self? If we must kill ourselves to get the knowledge of the self, we cannot be sure that we will, in fact, attain such knowledge.

Therefore, we will need a methodology which will enable us to have the same experience of destroying this physical body and yet not actually killing it! Hence the suggestion that we learn how to "die while living". We have been told by mystics that if we die while living, we would automatically destroy all the chakras, and our attention will come immediately to the point behind our eyes.... inside! When you withdraw your attention from the physical body and concentrate it behind the eyes, the process is the same as dying. You will become completely unaware of this physical body! Therefore, the mystics say don't destroy this physical body, simply "lose" awareness of it, by concentrating your attention at the point behind the eyes. If we are able to become completely unaware of this physical body, and hence the world outside, and still remain aware of the inner self, then we can—in effect—experience "dying while living"; and experience "life after death"! Therefore, let us see what it is which causes us to be aware of this physical body in the first place. We discover, upon examination, that what makes us aware of this physical body seems to be the very fact that we can "feel" the body itself. Indeed, all our actions which establish a relationship with the world around us, which make us aware of this world, must take place through the agency of the physical body. Therefore, we are "constantly" aware of this physical body and, as a result, come to identify ourselves with it. If we did not consciously "attend" to all the various things happening to the body, we would not be aware of it at all. If we did not put our attention into the sensory apparatus located in this body, not only would we lose awareness of this world, but we would also "lose" awareness of this physical body! We would become—literally speaking— dead!

It is, in fact, the blocking of the sensory systems located in the physical body, the actual withdrawal of our attention from the events happening through this body, that constitutes an effective method of meditation. But those of us who practise meditation know that the total withdrawal of attention is not so easy in practice, as it is in theory. Even if you are able to successfully withdraw your attention from the world by closing your eyes and ears, you will still remain conscious of the physical body. It is not as easy to sit still for two or three hours as it seems. There are all kinds of aches and pains. Sitting in meditation, you will eventually reach a point where it feels as if your legs are going to explode and that your bones are on fire! So please understand that it is not so easy to sit still for long periods of time necessary for effective withdrawal of attention.

How, then, do we withdraw our attention from the physical body itself, after we close our eyes and ears? The mystics' answer to this problem is that you must develop the capacity of staying at that place, in the physical body, where the conscious self resides. This place, the point from where all consciousness in the form of attention flows, is in the head—behind and between the two physical eyes! This point has often been called the "third eye" by many mystics, to distinguish it from the other two eyes. It is also sometimes called the "eye-focus" or "eye centre". It is from this point in the physical body that our attention travels outside—via the sensory system—and we become aware of the physical world and this physical body. Therefore, if we can successfully withdraw our scattered attention back to this point we will, in effect, "lose" awareness of the world as well as of the physical body itself! We will become aware of the "inner" self and the "inner" world. We are moving up to this focal point of consciousness every night when we sleep! It happens every night, and then we become unaware of the body and this world. The only problem is that we fail to hold our attention here had allow it to drop down to the throat centre where it then gets engulfed in a dream. Higher consciousness cannot be attained if the attention drops below the focal point at the eye-centre. To hold on to the focal point of consciousness behind the eyes, and not go to sleep, is the key to attaining higher consciousness.

The key to higher consciousness is the ability to concentrate your attention upon your ownself at this point, the eye-centre—behind the two physical eyes. If we slip into a sleep trance, we simply go into one of the lower chakras and will not experience a higher awareness or a higher consciousness. If we can maintain our wakefulness and still concentrate our attention upon ourselves, we will achieve a new experience—higher awareness! Once we are able to become unaware of the physical body, without taking any anaesthesia, without being knocked on the head, but by our own "Sadhana" (our own meditation), we discover that we possess immense energy and power of which we were unaware. This ability to concentrate attention on the self "within", behind the eyes at the "eye-centre", is no unique. It does not belong to only a few gifted people, but is available to each and everyone of us. Of course, there are many distractions which come in the way.

The most immediate problem that confronts us is that there is a process going on inside our heads called "thinking" that never seems to stop! Even when we close our eyes and ears, this thinking process—this thinking about the affairs of the world, our family and problems—continues to go on. In fact, scientists now believe that the thinking process never ceases! From birth to death, day or night, asleep or awake, conscious or unconscious . . . . this thinking process never stops. This, then, is the most difficult problem in the initial stage. What is "thinking"? Thinking is essentially a stream of thoughts made up of words that defines, describes and relates to some external experience of the physical self. Hence, whenever we think, we are in fact moving away from the eye-centre into phenomena! Therefore, thinking becomes "self-defeating". But alas, thinking cannot be stopped!

Now, how does the technology or methodology given by the mystics solve what seems to be an impossible dilemma? The mystics have devised a technique, a method called "bland word repetition" to overcome this obstacle. By the repetition of a set of words collectively referred to as a "mantra", they show their initiates how to pump these words into the thinking machine which, in turn, pumps out the thoughts of the affairs of the world! Since the connotation of the words contained in the thoughts running through the mind always refers to some external experience of the physical self, the mystics show us how—by substituting into the thinking process words which have NO outside connotation or reference—the outward flow of attention is stopped!

The next obstacle blocking our way in the journey back to the eye-centre is the problem of "visualization". You can go on repeating the mantra as fast and as loud as you like, but how can you stop the mind from seeing something? These mystics tell us that this problem also can be solved by adopting a method which they call "contemplation". Just as we are able, by substitution, to choke out the externalizing effects of the thinking process, we can, in turn, overcome the obstacles that arise from the distractions of external visualization by selecting a form or symbol that "pushes" our attention in, not out! The mystics say that the best object to select for our contemplation is something, in our external experience, which itself is continuously and singularly involved in the process of self-realization—that object is called the "Guru" or "Master". Even in this external experience, if you go to this object he will throw you back to yourself! His teachings will tell you to go back to the eye-centre. So even if, in the course of meditation, your attention travels away from the eye-centre to the visualization of this external form, you will again be pushed back inwardly.

To block out this second category of obstructions to the withdrawal of attention—the visualizations of the mind—we put before our mind's eye the form of the Guru. This aspect of the mystic methodology is also sometimes called "DHYAN". But even if you are able to block out the thoughts of the thinking process in the mind, by the repetition

100

of a mantra, and are able to also block out its visual distractions, by contemplating on the form of the Guru, what about the sounds that we are hearing all the time? Scientists have now discovered that there is some sound going on in the external universe all the time! Therefore, we can never experience a moment of external silence! At any moment, anywhere and any place we go, even if you sit in a cave with your ears plugged, you will STILL hear some kind of external sound! If nothing else, you will hear your own breathing or your heart beating! How, then, do we overcome this final obstruction to concentration which arises from the distractions of these external sounds? The principles of the method are once again the same. That is, we have to simply listen to a sound which is "within", not outside! Just as there are sounds of other things, there is also a "sound" of the self! This sound is audible and can be heard when our attention is properly focused.

There are five forms of this sound in every human being. The mystics have referred to it by various names in their writings. It is the "WORD" of the Bible; the "kalma" of the Holy Quran, the "NAD" of the Vedas, the "Shabd" or "Sound current" in the terminology of contemporary mysticism. So, by focusing our attention on this sound, we are able to overcome the last obstacle to withdrawal of our attention back to the focal point of consciousness behind the eyes.

What happens when we are able to do all these things?

When you withdraw your attention, through meditation, to the third eye centre, behind the two physical eyes, you will gradually become unaware of the extremities of the body! If you are able to sit for a sufficiently long period of time, in the right posture for meditation, and concentrate

101

your attention at the point behind the eyes, after a while you will lose awareness of your feet! You won't feel them! Sometimes in the beginning of this practice, you have to open your eyes to look and see that they have not disappeared! You become completely unaware of them! A while later, the hands are gone! And if you are persistent and have the patience, you will then notice that your legs, arms and so on also disappear from your field of awareness! When you lose awareness of them, then you will experience a very strange thing. The body awareness completely disappears, and you feel that you are just awareness alone without any vehicle! When the attention is withdrawn from the bottom of the body, you have the strange sensation of floating in the air! You realize that it was only because you could "feel", through attention, the ground on which you sit; that you have the experience of "gravity" . . . of being on the ground! The moment attention is withdrawn from the bottom of the torso, you discover that "YOU" are not sitting on the ground at all! You will have the feeling of being in mid-air; you will experience . . . "levitation". You feel that, somehow or other, you have "risen", but you are still in the body which is still sitting there in the same place!

If you continue withdrawing your attention further upwards, it eventually reaches the throat centre. You will then become completely unconscious and unaware of the body, and the light coming from the third eye centre floods you! Eventually, when you are able to fully complete the process of withdrawal of attention to the third eye-centre, you are able to see the gate . . . the tenth door! The door that leads into this temple of the Lord! Many yogis have preferred to travel along these chakras, as they have spent too many years and too much effort involved with the principles of energy. Therefore, they would rather awaken the energy centres one after the other. As a result, they are able to develop yogic and supernatural powers.

But the highest mystics, those who are interested in journeys that go far beyond the entrance to the temple, have recommended that we need not waste our time going through each of the chakras. They say that we should practise the art of withdrawing the attention "directly" to the eye centre. When the attention is withdrawn to the third eye-centre, it opens up into a region which is full of light and sound. The light and sound within us is so beautiful that it is impossible to describe it in words! The sound is like that of a big bell. Its peels are so loud and the music is so beautiful that anyone who has had this experience can never forget it! It is not just a sound, it is a power that pulls you. It is like a conscious being! It is like a friend. It "IS" the source of consciousness; it is the sound which makes you conscious! And this entire episode takes place when you are able to withdraw your attention back to the eye centre. It is what would happen if you died. Therefore, it is referred to by the mystics as the art of "dying while living".

When you die, the same thing happens but then you are not able to come back and share this knowledge with anybody. But if you could die, while still living in this body, then you would be able to describe the journey within. Therefore, we have to simulate this dying while still being alive through the use of the mystic methodology. What happens when you die? When a person is dying, you will notice that he becomes unconscious of the parts of his body. When a person is dying, the first experience is that of losing consciousness of the feet, hands and so on. He is still able to talk but does not know what has happened to his feet and hands. Then gradually, the person becomes unconscious of the whole body and no longer knows "where" he or she is! But he is still able to talk! The "head" is still there and it is the last part of the physical body to drop out of awareness. When this happens, the person is said to have died! Then

103

there is no life left. In the same way, if we can simulate death, that is, withdraw our attention from the body in the same manner—from the extremities up to the head—we can have the same experience of "going within" . . . the experience of life after death! All this can be accomplished by the use of attention.

Human attention is the most wonderful gift that has been given to us. Whatever we place our attention on, that becomes real for us! In fact, the only things we are ever able to experience are those things on which we put our attention! If you put all of your attention on this book, the rest of the room in which you are now sitting will simply disappear. When the attention is again unconcentrated, that is "scattered", you will again become aware of the rest of the room around you. Great marksmen, who are able to hit the bull's-eye all the time, have practised the art of "focusing" attention to such an extent that they do not "see" anything else except the target they want to hit. If they allowed themselves to become aware of anything else, they would not hit the target. So they are trained to practise the art of concentration of attention in such a way that they do not see anything else! And whenever you concentrate your attention on something, you will automatically lose awareness of the other things going on around you. It is the use of attention in this manner which enables us to do this wonderful thing called "dying while living". We are conscious of our hands and feet and this entire world simply because of the use of attention. Our attention is scattered throughout the body and from there—via the organs of perceptions—the whole world comes into being.

If we can imagine this head of ours as a room, and we are sitting in the centre of it, and if we then put all of our attention here, we will become completely unaware of our hands and feet and gradually the rest of the physical body. The experience will be identical to the process of death! And when the attention is withdrawn up to the waist, you will have the sensation of flying! You will not know where "you" are, even whether you have a body or not! When the attention reaches the centre behind the eyes, you will discover that "you" are separate from the body.... you will "see" your own body separate from you! It is a tremendous experience. You will be able to see your physical body from the outside just like everybody else sees it. You can see your own physical body just sitting there!

With your astral body, you are able to walk through walls, you can fly, you can have the same feelings of touching, tasting, smelling, seeing and so on while the physical body is still just sitting there! Then one wonders, "Why have I been calling it 'me'?" "Who am I?" "I thought that was me!" It is a strange and very frightening experience to see your body separate from you! The first sense that you will use will be that of sight. You will be able to "see" independently of the physical eyes which are closed! Then you will discover that you are able to walk away and "leave" the body sitting there! It is as if you are stepping into a different world! This ability to use the sense perception, without using the physical body, is called "astral travel". When this complete complex of sense perception moves away from the physical body and yet continues to function, you discover that you are able to touch, taste, smell and so on with much greater clarity and scope! In this astral state, you move just as if you were walking with feet. But when you look, you will see that you really don't have any feet! And when you start to run you discover that you can run very, very fast; that you can move at a velocity greater than the velocity of light itself! What's more, you can run right through walls and everything else! It is a very strange but wonderful experience. If you want to see what is happening in the other room, you can just look "intently" and you can see what is going on. In the astral body, you will discover you have faculties that you never dreamt of! Anybody can do this! You can do it also, by the simple method of using your attention to focus away from the physical experience and onto the point from where the attention flows. But there is one big problem. The problem is that when the attention rises above the throat, there is the experience of dying . . . . real dying! One becomes afraid, and out of this fear pumps his attention back into the whole body.

All of us are really afraid of dying. But we really do not realize how much, until death actually comes. Therefore, when we are able to simulate the experience of death by withdrawing the attention to the eye centre, we naturally become very frightened and start to panic! This may be the "real" thing! This fear comes because we really are dying! The soul really does separate from the body! Although actually, the physical body is not dead. We are merely shifting our focus of attention to a point where we can segregate it from the body. There are vital centres within the body that continue to support its life functions while the astral body takes over as the vehicle of our conscious experience. At the eye-centre, we are able to segregate the astral body from the physical body, while its life remains sustained by these energy centres. Life remains in the physical body in the same way as it is maintained when we are in deep sleep or in a trance. But because of the fear that accompanies the experience of coming to the eye centre, it is advised that you attempt this exercise only under the guidance of a trained teacher; one who is a master in this art and has himself made this journey many, many times. Then it becomes very safe and once you have practised it, you are able to leave the body and travel at will for as long as you like! You will discover that there are many different and new experiences available while in this astral state of being.

One of the experiences available is the ability to read other people's minds and thoughts! As a result, your ability to communicate is greatly enhanced because you "know" what the other person is thinking about! You are then able to respond "precisely" to his need, which often startles and amazes him! You will be able to see his doubts, his true emotions and so on! It is all very, very amazing. In this astral state, you also discover that everything you are seeing around you is being seen without there being any light! Here, in the physical state, you cannot see anything or anybody unless there is light! If the light is turned off in the room in which you are sitting, everything will become "invisible" to you because you need external light in order to see. But in the astral state of being, you can switch off the light and you STILL will be able to see everything! Everybody and everything, viewed from this state of being, seems to have a light of its own! They can be seen without the need of any external light! That is why in this state, things and people are often said to be "luminous" and "radiant".

There is an internal illumination in everything and everyone! It is an extraordinary experience and for those who have it for the first time, they think that it is the final and ultimate experience! "We have found heaven" they say. We have found paradise....we have found everything! It is at this point that the teacher, the master, appears in his own "radiant" form and says, "I have brought you here to start the spiritual journey, not to end it."

XII

THE MASTER A MUST

WE now come to a point in our analysis of the journey towards self-realization about which there is not much understanding: the role of the master in the quest for self-realization. The word "master" has been used in many different senses. Indeed, there is a great deal of controversy on whether or not a master is even needed for such a journey. It is only when one reaches the eye centre that the need for a master really becomes necessary. Up to this point, withdrawal of attention is easy. Anybody can do it! It is not something very difficult. But, upon reaching this point, your progress will simply stop. The experience of reaching the eye centre is so beautiful that you will no longer have any "urge" to rise to the higher states of consciousness. You will feel that this is the end. And it is here that you need the master to convince you that, "no, this is just the beginning". He "pushes" you forward. He takes you on a flight throughout this entire universe! You will then discover that there are many more worlds existing which are far more beautiful than this world known to us. You are amazed to find that there are many MORE people who have attained a higher level of awareness than you had ever imagined! We think only a few rare souls have attained this higher state of awareness. In fact, this world in which we live is simply a replica of these higher worlds. You will discover that the events happening on this physical

108

plane of consciousness are nothing more than a replay! You find out that the "film" of this physical life is made there, and is then projected through time, space and causation, onto this physical experience! The space-time continuum outside is simply a screen on which consciousness is projecting a film already made at the astral level of consciousness! On this plane, we are able to actually see these films being loaded into consciousness at this physical level.

You can see how, in the future, we will be able to plug ourselves into each other and transfer our thoughts and feelings in a few seconds! Since the mode of communication at the astral level is that of telepathy, it will eventually be reflected at the physical plane of consciousness over here! We will then call it a scientific discovery. At this level of consciousness, you will be able to see everything that is going to happen on this physical plane for the next 2,000 years! You will see all of these events there. It is a fantastic experience! And it is the spiritual master who makes it possible for you to see all of this. He is able to give you instructions on how, by the use of one's own personal consciousness, this region of awareness can be attained. In fact, he will accompany you throughout your whole journey inside consciousness. You will also begin to notice how the lords of these regions respect him; how they show a certain type of reverence and honour to him which they do not show to anyone else. And you begin to wonder what is so special about him. He is just a co-traveller with me. He is simply a guide who has brought me to this level. Why is he being shown so much respect? But the people at this higher level of awareness "know" who he is. They know that he belongs to a "higher" region. The master is now "teaching" you in a different way than he did on this physical plane.

At the physical level, the master teaches you how to "go within"; how to trigger the experience of reaching the astral state of being. Once you have been able to achieve this, he must then take you out of this state because you will like it so much that you will not want to leave it! He has to somehow or other persuade you that there is still something better than this. He has a very hard time doing this because, in spite of everything he says, you do not want to go on.

The astral region is so beautiful and satisfying that you do not ever want to leave it! It is everything you have hoped for and you do not want anything more! But the master goes on insisting that this is not the end and you must go on. He then takes you to still higher realms of consciousness by showing you how to withdraw your attention, through the process of listening to the "Sound Current", the sound of the self that I mentioned in the previous chapter. This process then enables you to withdraw your attention from the astral body itself and takes you into the region of pure mind! There, the senses are no longer necessary! In this state of consciousness, it is no longer necessary to have the "power to see" in order to see! It is no longer necessary to have the "power to hear" in order to hear, and so on. At this level of consciousness you acquire the capacity to have "direct perception", — the ability to have experiences directly with the mind! You are able to enter the region of the "universal mind", the "causal region", where all things and events have their origin! This causal region is simply the region of "pure" mind, where neither the physical nor the astral body are required!

There are hardly any words that can describe the experience of this state of being! It is really impossible to give a description of it! Yet, something must be said. But first, let me clarify one very important point. These regions are not one above the other. You don't have to go from here to there! All these different regions are in the same place! They are "within" your own consciousness! Even

110

this physical world, which we see around us, is within CONSCIOUSNESS from where we project it outside! Even the dream world which we experience when we slip below this wakeful level of consciousness is contained within this same consciousness! Therefore, we do not actually "go" anywhere to have these experiences of higher regions. They automatically come into being when we shift our focus of attention! This must be clearly understood throughout this description of the journey to higher regions.

When we enter into the causal region, we are able to have the experience of "total time"! In the astral region, we were surprised to discover that time could be suspended! In this physical region, time cannot be held. You are having some nice experience and you want to "hold" on to it, but this cannot be done at this physical level. However, it can be done at the astral level. At the causal level, you can not only suspend time, but you are able to travel backward and forward as well! If you want, you can move backwards into the past to re-experience your happiest moments. Not through memory, but through the "actual" re-experience of the event! If there is some experience happening to you that you do not particularly care for, you can "leap" over it and continue travelling until you reach an experience of your liking! It is an incredible experience. At the causal level of consciousness, time becomes mobile. You can move through time in any direction that you like. You have the ability to go through past, present and future experiences at will! Along with the nature of time, the whole concept of reality changes!

We discover that what we thought was the beginning of an event is not so, because this experience can be had at "any time" throughout the flow of time! When you can travel in any direction in the time continuum, where is the beginning? You can make any part of time the beginning,

111

the middle or the end! This new and unique ability completely overwhelms and fills us with elation. Then, we become anxious to know more about the nature of this new reality we are experiencing.

At the causal level, we also discover that the reason we were able to communicate through telepathy at the astral level was because there is only ONE mind! We discover that ALL thoughts of ALL people were there inside one single "universal" mind! Entering into the causal state of being, we acquire access to ALL thoughts being had by all minds....throughout the entire spectrum of time! I cannot really describe the impact of the realization that what you thought was "your" mind and "his" mind, were simply fragments of a single mind! As a result of this experience, all misunderstandings, all problems in human relationships immediately disappear!

At the causal level of consciousness, another very interesting thing also takes place. We discover that all past actions, all future actions and all current actions are being manufactured here! We are able to see how the "Law of Karma" operates! At this physical level of consciousness, we do not know if a certain event which occurred happened because of something we had done a few moments before or because of something we did ten lives ago! In fact, we are not even sure that there is such a thing as a "past" lifetime! At this physical level, we have absolutely no knowledge about matters such as these. But when we are able to so into the causal region of consciousness, we are capable of seeing our entire lifetime as well as that of any other person we want! The experiences which we get, upon entering the causal region, are so immense, so expansive and total, that no one can believe that there could be any experience higher than this!

Even the most knowledgeable person, someone who has made a very deep study of the levels of human consciousness before making the journey, upon reaching this level, finds it impossible to conceive of anything higher than it! The experience is too grand and too immense for anyone to intellectually comprehend it. And when it happens to you, you are really convinced that "This is it"! And again, the master, whom you now see in his causal form, must somehow take you still higher.

"You are still in the realm of the mind", he tells you. "This is not the end of the journey....we have still a very long way to go! Consciousness transcends mind and you must go beyond this region." But the experience of this region is so tremendous that we refuse to believe even the master! The master has a very, very difficult time in persuading us to go beyond the causal level. Therefore, a very long period of time is spent in this region. Incidentally, when I say a lot of time, I am not referring to a few years. I am referring to much longer spans of time! Hundreds of thousands of years are sometimes spent in this region! We cannot believe that there is anything beyond this region, and the enjoyment of it is so fulfilling that we flatly refuse to make any attempt to continue our journey. It is only through spiritual force that the master is able to take us up to the next region of consciousness where even the universal mind gets left behind — the "pure spiritual region".

Once we reach the pure spiritual region, we discover that it was the mind itself which was creating time! All events, whether they were total or not, were being sustained in a time frame created by the mind. Even if you could move in either direction on this continuum, it was still "within" time! At the causal level, we are not able to cross time itself. This capacity comes only after we are able to rise into the pure spiritual state of being! It is really impossible to give any description of this region. Those souls who are able to experience this level of consciousness have not been able to describe it with words. At best, they are only able to describe it in a negative sense — "NETI NETI", not this....not that! Therefore, strictly speaking, I should end here because nothing more can be said! One of India's greatest mystics, Sant Kabir, has written a very beautiful book which is an account of a conversation with his principal disciple, Dharmadas. The book is called "Anuraag Sagar" — the Ocean of Love! In it, Dharmadas asks Kabir to say something about the higher regions beyond the mind.

> "You have been lecturing to me for a long time about the higher level of consciousness; about a higher way of seeing things. Why don't you tell me what this is really about? What is this higher consciousness?" .... Kabir replies, "Dharmadas, how can I say anything about it to you? I can't describe it with the words of this world. How can I explain to you that there is a state of consciousness where there is no time? How would you comprehend it? How can you comprehend a state of being where there is no time and no space? But these are only words! They are not the experience! We can go on and on repeating that the experience is one of timelessness and spacelessness but it will not be a description of this region!"

And then Kabir goes on to tell Dharmadas, in a storybook fashion, the whole tale of creation relating it to the worldly life here. It is one of the greatest books ever written.

When the causal region is traversed, and you are able to enter into a higher level of conscious experience, then alone are you able to realize that TIME is not an indispensable coordinate of experience, that one can have experience

114

WITHOUT time! You are able to have the experience of "timeless" time! This timeless time is where all time is total! All time is existing in ONE SINGLE MOMENT and you need not move backwards or forward! The entire scope of all experiences available within time is "capsuled" into a single, timeless moment! This experience is impossible to describe! I don't know why I am even trying to say anything about it! I am just trying to give some idea, however inadequate, about the incredible nature of the pure spiritual experience. It is an experience where time need not be extended in order to have personal experience.

All experiences are condensed at this level of consciousness. At this level, one has an intense longing to be "ONE" with everyone....to "LOVE" everyone! Everything is known instantly.... "INTUITIVELY"! No time is required! This timeless, spaceless experience occurs when we are able to enter into this spiritual region existing one step above the causal region. At this level, we transcend everything relevant to all known reality. Our experience becomes permanent! It never suffers death, it never changes, it remains exactly the same as it always was, has been and always will be! At this level, we discover that our nature is the same as that of God Himself! That MAN IS GOD! He is made of the same stuff of which God is made but has been completely ignorant of this fact. Man is a seed — the seed of God.

And when man reaches the pure spiritual level of consciousness, he blossoms....the "God" in him becomes manifest. The fragrance of divineness is released because "Godliness" has bloomed in you, and you become so fulfilled and joyous that you have no desire or need to go anywhere else! We then thank our spiritual master for bringing us to this "highest" level of consciousness. But he says, "No, this is still not the end of our journey! You

115

have only discovered your own self, you have yet to discover "GOD HIMSELF!"

When we transcend the pure spiritual region we are able to cross the last barrier....the barrier of "Individuation"! Even this feeling that there can be more than one soul, that you are simply one of many billions of other souls, is an illusion! We discover that at the level of "total consciousness", we are able to transcend the experience of individuation....the experience of "ego"! At this level of consciousness, no time, not even timeless time, exists! This state of totality of consciousness contains all experiences from the lowest dream up to the very highest and is being experienced by ONE SINGLE CONSCIOUSNESS....your own! It is difficult to explain how the "whole" of experience is fused together into one total experience. It is unconfined, unlimited and has no time or space! I am not sure you can even understand this concept of unlimited consciousness without time and without space! But this is the experience one gets when one reaches the level of total consciousness. At this level of consciousness, you discover that you have unlimited possibilities, that you are "ONE" with the creator....one with God Himself! Hence, upon attaining this level of consciousness, every person — with no exception — has proclaimed the same thing...."AHAM BRAHMASMI".... "I am God"! It simply means they have "realized" that their seed is no more a seed, it has disappeared into the soil of existence, and they have come to the ultimate blossoming ....to the "peak" of creation.

At the level of total consciousness, you are able to have "total experience"! Total experience means ALL experiences, not just the "highest" experience. This must be clearly understood. The highest experience is LOWER than the experience of totality, and when anyone attains this level

116

of total consciousness, he CONTINUES to be aware of all of the levels of consciousness below, whether he is here or there. At this level, your experience becomes one of "symphonic consciousness"!

People very often wonder whether those who have reached this level of consciousness have to "come down" and "go up" in order to know what is happening at the various planes of reality. They don't! They are totally aware of EVERYTHING at every level of human awareness! This, then, is a brief description of what lies within every human being's own consciousness! I have tried to describe the variety of experiences available in human consciousness as best as I could. The language, any language, is completely inadequate! It is something which cannot be described in words. But I have to try to say something about these things because very few people have ever been told of such human possibilities. The secrets of your own consciousness have been kept hidden from you!

As a result, a deep feeling of worthlessness surrounds your existence. Society has conditioned you to feel very negative towards yourself! You have been conditioned to believe that your worth is not intrinsic. You are asked to "prove" yourself; to achieve success; to make a lot of money! You are asked to "earn" respectability and prestige! You must prove you are worth something! And this idea of success goes on torturing you throughout your whole life. Hence, the deep feeling that "I am worthless as a human being unless I prove otherwise" destroys all the beauty of human experience. But, when you are able to realize that you are one with God—one with the Creator Himself—this becomes proof enough of your worth. No other proof is needed. You discover the infinite immensity of your own consciousness. For the first time, you are able to really love "yourself" which is the only way you can ever love "God". Therefore, the greatest fortune that can ever befall a human being in this world is to be initiated by a perfect master, who will then give him the "key to the kingdom of God" .... the key to higher consciousness.

XIII

▼

INITIATION

THE word "initiation" is used all over the world to indicate the entry or introduction of someone into a new discipline or subject. However, "spiritual initiation" of the perfect masters that will be examined in this chapter introduces us into "higher awareness" and takes us into higher levels of consciousness! It is not simply an introduction into a new discipline or subject—it means much more than this. From the very beginning, I want to make it absolutely clear that a very large number of initiations going on, especially in this country, are not the kind of initiations that I consider authentic and real. Today, you can "purchase" initiation into many cults and various kinds of yogic practices by simply paying a fee! This is not the "spiritual" initiation of which I am speaking, when I refer to initiation by a perfect living master. A long time ago, initiation was not so easy. It could not be purchased for a few dollars! It was very difficult to obtain. A seeker would have to sometimes wait for years to be initiated! Some were made to wait for almost the whole of their lives, because unless they were "ready" they would not be accepted by the masters. This waiting itself became a way of testing the "maturity" of a soul! The more impatient the mind, the less mature was the soul. In other cases, a seeker was not even allowed to ask any questions—none!

Sometimes, you would be made to wait for five or ten days before you could even ask a single question! But today, we can hardly wait even an hour before we attack the masters with our questions! An hour seems to be the longest we can stay with a trend of thought! Whereas, in the old days, you would be made to "hold" the thought; to stay with it until it matured, and then, like a ripe fruit, it would fall away of its own accord! No "real" questions can be answered by words. Questions can only be answered by an "experience"; by something existential . . . but never through the intellect! This simple waiting, unquestioned waiting, the reliance upon the Master to pick the right moment, would prepare the seekers of that time to make tremendous progress when they were finally initiated! But today, the whole thing has become a different matter because no one is willing to wait. We have become such victims of time, that to wait for even a single moment is impossible! As a result of this "time" consciousness, we cannot afford to "waste" our time when we come across a perfect master. He will make us wait! And, the mind will ask, "What are you doing? Why are you wasting your time with this man? Is that which he is offering you really worth the wait? Will it really lead you to anything?" But this waiting is the price you will have to pay—and one has to pay a price for everything!

However, we are only willing to pay with money, not with faith, and trust!

Because of this "hurry-up" attitude, which is characteristic of these modern times, initiation from the perfect masters has become almost impossible! Full of impatience, ignorance and lack of faith, we rush to such a master, and ask him, "Will you initiate me?" But, even during this brief asking, we are still on the run! Traditional initiation has become almost impossible, but there is still no alternative to some kind of initiation! Initiation is still needed! To meet this need, there are thousands of phony gurus and Swami "this" or Swami "that" who are willing to sell you a "QUICK-FIX" initiation for a fee! Today, in the name of mysticism, something pseudo—something false—is being sold. America is full of gurus who are selling you something which has nothing to do with spirituality. Now, this is not the kind of initiation I am referring to as initiation by a perfect living master. However, even if one does have the patience to wait and trust . . . to "surrender"—there still remains another problem in being initiated by a perfect master . . . their initiation is NOT done at the physical level at all!

There is no such thing as initiation at this physical level so far as a perfect master is concerned! The perfect master operates from the higher levels of consciousness and initiates us at a level of consciousness higher than this wakeful state. When a perfect master initiates you, he creates a connection between you and his higher form at the next higher level of consciousness. No perfect master ever initiates his disciples at this physical plane! The "real" initiation takes place at the astral level within, from where he operates; from where he connects his "spiritual form" to ours. He does not believe in teaching any new system of rituals and ceremonies. He does not propagate any new practices or methods of worship. We have already been confused enough by all these things. We have been praying and worshipping the Lord for thousands of years in thousands of different ways.

Therefore, the perfect master simply says, "Worship Him in whatever manner you like." There is no harm in praying to the Lord in any manner you desire, because your relationship with Him is direct! In fact, prayer with words and so on is not even necessary! But if you like, you may pray and worship in whatever fashion you think is correct and effective; it hardly makes any difference. To whom are you praying anyway? You and the Lord are ONE! You are

121

simply "talking" to your own self! Prayer is really one of the most misunderstood notions found in religion. It is as if you are praying before a mirror, seeing your own face, kneeling down before your own image, begging for favours! There is nothing in the mirror except your own reflection! Similarly, there is no distinction between that which we call God and our own self, and all prayers—however beautiful they may be—are, therefore, regressive. Your own consciousness is the "creator" of this entire experience of the world which you are having!

When the perfect master initiates you, he will take you to a level much higher than prayers, rituals and worship! He enables you to "personally" reach a level of consciousness much higher than this wakeful physical level at which your search for God-realization was confined to rituals and ceremonies! Therefore, his initiation will have nothing to do with religion. Initiation by a perfect master does not require you to change or drop your religion; to change your form of worship or concept of God. Nor does it require you to make any changes in your cultural background or nationality.

It requires only a change in your attitude! A change from the attitude that "I know everything" to that of "I don't know anything". Your so-called "knowledge" is an illusion of the mind that you must leave! It is fictitious; just a creation of words; a fantasy, made of the same "stuff" that dreams are made of! You will then come to realize that "you don't understand anything; you cannot understand anything. Your consciousness is confined to this dream-like physical level of consciousness. You are part and parcel of this physical world which is simply a creation of your own mental projections! You are dreaming all the time, even while fully awake!" This change, from that of deep metaphysical sleep to that of seeking and searching for "reality", is the only change required for initiation from a perfect master. But if there is no "outward" change required for initiation by a perfect master, then what "is" initiation? What happens when you are initiated by a perfect master?

When you are initiated by the perfect master, all your "karma" is destroyed! There is no new karma added, and you are liberated from the clutches of actions and their consequences! To fully appreciate the significance of this event, you must clearly understand what this "Law of Karma" and its relationship to an individual's spiritual plight are. The very first thing that must be understood is that karma is a state of consciousness, and is a function of the human mind. We call this part of the human mind, which is exposed to the impression coming into its field of awareness, the "Antahkarana". The Antahkarana is the sensitive part of the mind which picks up the impressions of our conscious experiences. These impressions are called "Samskaras". These samskaras are simply the previous impressions left by what we have experienced in consciousness. Once these impressions are picked up by the human mind, they are retained and our future course of experience is then guided by them. It is this process by which the mind picks up these impressions and then releases them back into our experiences to be worked out, that is called the "Law of Karma"!

Therefore, Karma is entirely mental! We create Karma with our mind and we also work it out through the mind! A mental decision may or may not be followed by a physical act, but Karma is still there! Karma need not always be worked out through our physical actions. In fact, if the mind is unaware of a certain activity, then there is no Karma. But if it IS aware of something mentally, but NO physical act follows, Karma is still created! Karma, then, is merely the "retention" of previous memories, experiences and their

123

impressions within the human mind. It is the working out of these impressions in our present and future decision-making processes based upon our previous experiences.

Therefore, we are bound to act in a certain way because of these previous experiences and impressions. We are "destined" to do certain things, therefore some of these impressions are called "Fate Karma" . . . "Pralabdha Karma"—Karma over which we have no control. When we have cleared up these impressions and start to create new ones, then these new impressions are called "New Karma"; Karma that will form the basis of "Fate Karma" for the future. This new Karma is also sometimes called "Kriyaman Karma". But how, you may ask, can we "jam" up all of the activity, all of the follow-up actions of our Karma within the scope of a single life-time? The answer is that it is held in "storage" for a future life! The concept of Karma is, therefore, tied up with the concept of reincarnation.

The concept of reincarnation is that this "overflow" of Karma is being in reserve in the same Antahakarana . . . . the same mind! Since the mind cannot work out each impression that comes into it within a single lifetime, it stores these unused impressions in its sensitive part, to be worked out in a future lifetime! This third type of Karma which is held in reserve for distribution in a future life, is called "reserved Karma". It is also sometimes referred to as "Sanchit Karma". All three kinds of Karma, briefly described as Pralabdha, Kriyaman and Sanchit, become a heavy load on our consciousness and make it impossible to rise above this physical level of consciousness! Therefore, you can now understand and appreciate the great significance of getting initiation from a perfect master! The master, by using the force of his own consciousness, frees us from the mind and from our load of Karma! Initiation by the perfect master is the only process by which a human being can escape from the law of Karma. What goes on thereafter is just "mock" Karma created to preserve the pattern of experience in this life. There is no new Karma! You are liberated from the realms of Karma! Initiation by a perfect master is not just an external ceremony!

If a person who claims to be a guru simply gives you a few words to repeat, saying "This is the mantra, now I have given you initiation", you can be sure you have been given nothing! If he has not linked you with his own spiritual force within; not severed your connection with the negative power of time, which sustains your load of Karma; if he does not do all this, then he has not been of any help to you! Therefore, initiation by a perfect living master is the greatest event that can happen to you in this world! It is something which angels, rulers of higher realms, souls who are governing this entire creation . . . those who themselves are creators of regions of consciousness, are waiting and hoping for! They are all waiting for a connection with this "spiritual force" which is a direct link . . . to the "totality" of consciousness! Therefore, when a seeker is "ready", he is then picked up and initiated . . . he is "CHOSEN", and once you are initiated by a perfect master, he will simply laugh at all the efforts you are still making to reach the higher levels of consciousness! All the yoga and meditation you are doing is just being done out of past habits! The truth is: even if you make numerous efforts, they are not going to take you anywhere!

God-realization does not fall within the laws of causation! God-realization is not causal, it is "acausal" . . . without any cause! This has to be clearly understood! The tendency of the "logical" person or a "rational" man is to either decide that God-realization is causal (and that by his

125

effort he can achieve it), or that it is acausal, (it happens only when it happens . . . of its own accord, and there is no need to make efforts)! This is how intellect will divide the reality of our spiritual plight. But, in both ways, you will miss the point . . . the "whole" point.

If you think it is causal and you make efforts to do "great sadhana", you will fail because it is not causal. Yet, if you conclude that it is acausal, and hence, there is no need to make efforts, or why bother, again you will miss! You will have to make all the effort possible, because you are "prepared" through your efforts to be "receptive" when it happens! The reality is: God-realization is acausal. It will "happen" to you; it is not going to happen through your efforts. Your efforts will simply make you "ready"; make you open and vulnerable to the master. The master, seeing the validity and sincerity of your efforts—out of compassion and love—draws you within and takes you on a flight from the known to the unknown . . . from the self to the total self—to God-realization!

"Come to the edge," he said. They said: "We are afraid." "COME TO THE EDGE!", he said. They came. He PUSHED them . . . and they flew.

(APOLLINAIRE)

XIV

HOW DO WE COMMUNICATE?

WE communicate with each other, and with nature, in many ways. But the most common form of communication between two human beings is through the use of words . . . language. Words, in any language, are simply "sounds" and then meanings are given to these sounds based on our own personal association of ideas with them! Words are nothing more than "phonetic" symbols which have a meaning simply because we have associated these sounds with a certain experience. And, if the phonetic sound is repeated again and again in relation to the same experience, we give it a meaning related to that experience. If I see an object and I call it a "chair" and keep on saying it is a "chair" every time I see it, then the word "chair" takes on the meaning and connotation of the chairs that I have seen. Other people may also have used the word "chair" in relation to some type of object that they call "chair". Therefore, when I say "chair", the other person who hears the word "chair" does not understand the same thing!

No two persons can understand a word in exactly the same way because no two persons have seen exactly the same object! If we each see one chair and then use the word "chair", the limitation is caused by the type of object that we have seen! And even when we see a larger number of chairs with different shapes and sizes, we still use the word "chair"! However, the word "chair" then means not only that one chair which we saw, but the "idea" of a chair! It will then also mean all the chairs seen by us whenever we use the word "chair"! And the person who hears the word "chair" will not see that particular chair. He will "see" the chair which is an accumulated "idea" of all of the chairs which he has seen! And since no two persons can have the same identical experience of the objects to which we give names, no two persons will have the same meaning for one word! This is the greatest drawback in communicating with language.

In the case of objects such as chairs, tables, trees, animals, and so on, it is not such a great problem. But, when we start talking of intangibles and abstract subjects like love, jealousy, hatred, God, religion, meditation, and so on, the difficulty increases because these words have completely different meanings for different people! When two people talk about "love", they do not realize that they are talking about two different things! And there is no way for them to even know that their "understanding" of the word "LOVE" is different! Each one will use the word "love" in the sense in which he knows; the listener will interpret the word "LOVE" in the sense in which he understands it! The two of them will have completely different meanings for this word, and there is no possibility for either of them to know that his understanding is different from the others! But, we know that since the connotation given by the association of ideas has to be different; since human experience is not identical, they could not possibly have the same meaning! Yet, knowing that the language we use, the "words" that we use, cannot mean the same things . . . we still keep on trying to communicate with words! Therefore, whenever the tangibles and

128

the intangibles intermingle and we still try to use language, we run into a lot of difficulty. You will find that when two people misunderstand each other, they do so because they never understood each other in the first place! There was no scope for understanding! They discover their misunderstanding the hard way, when they move from the intangible to the tangible! When the "tangible" is brought before them, they will say "this is not what I meant"! When we talk of an intangible thing, like love or hatred, and when it is translated into real situations, into an "actual" movement of people towards love or hatred, only then do we discover the misunderstanding! It is also a strange thing to notice that, the moment we try to explain too much, we are misunderstood all the more! The more words we use, the more we are misunderstood! It seems it should be the other way around! But, in fact, if you use fewer words, then the chances of misunderstanding are actually less!

The majority of misunderstandings in our human relationships have arisen from the excessive use of words. This is a very serious handicap and limitation in communication between human beings. The other difficulty in communication is that all communication at this physical level of consciousness is being done by the mind alone! We are being educated and sent to colleges and universities to undergo an educational process, which believes exclusively in sharpening the instrument of the mind and analysis. We are trained how to analyze, how to use the power of reasoning, how to use logic, how to think; but not how to "feel" —— how to use our hearts! This makes it even more difficult, almost impossible, to communicate with each other! We have been trained only how to use words. The result is that you create doubt and confusion in the mind of the person who is listening to you! This "word processing" which is being done by the mind, through which human beings are communicating with each other, is constantly beset by doubts and uncertainties! It is the nature of the human mind to use this process, and whenever two persons talk to each other, with the mind, they end up in a state of doubt and uncertainty.

In fact, the more educated the mind of a person is, the more likely is he to use phrases such as, "I am not sure", "maybe", "perhaps", "I don't think so", "I do not know" and so on! Just listen to the conversation of the so-called "educated" people. The more "highly" educated the person is, the more he has been trained in the art of using his mind and intellect, the more he will use such expressions which show that he is not sure, . . . that he is uncertain! This is natural. Because the more you use the mind and the abilities of deductive and inductive logic, the more uncertain you are bound to become! And when you are so uncertain in presenting your own point of view, there is every reason for the person who listens to you to also become uncertain! And now, a very interesting chain reaction takes place.

When a person speaks in such a way that his uncertainties are expressly included in his language, then the other person will begin to have doubts about the person's "motive" and reason for making the statement. This kind of communication creates a "chain reaction" of doubt and, therefore, ... fear! And when you make someone afraid of you, you cannot communicate with him! So linguistic communication between two persons creates this problem of doubt, fear and, ultimately, hatred and misunderstanding! You see this all the time! When you see two people misunderstanding each other, hating each other, and when you, as a friend, intervene and listen to both parties, you discover that it was not either one's fault! It was due to lack of communication! There was a "breakdown" in communication since both of them were trying to communicate with their minds!

130

This is the biggest problem in trying to communicate with the mind. But is there any other way in which we can communicate? If language — communication with the mind, logic and reasoning — is no good, ... then how do we communicate? If there are limitations to communication, how do we overcome these limitations?

There is a solution. Each human being, fortunately, does not only have a language and a mind to use but also has that wonderful thing which we call the "soul" or "spirit". The soul or spirit performs certain functions which are not performed by the mind. All the functions of the mind are limited. And, this limitation creates difficulties that I have mentioned earlier. What does the human soul or the spirit do, which is distinct from the mind? It has the ability to be "pure" consciousness and have a look at the mind! It can step aside and listen to the thoughts of the mind; it can see the mind at work; it can see the mind performing the function of communication. It is that part of human awareness that can "watch" all of this going on! This is the spirit, the soul, ... the "self". It is what we are trying to discover when we ask, "Who am I?" The self is the basis of consciousness, the "motor force" for all conscious functions and we distinguish it from the mind because of its higher functions.

Now there is a higher means of communication between human beings, and that is through the use of the soul or the spirit. In fact, there is no better means of communication between two human beings than communication through the "spiritual" process; through love; through intuition; . . . . through beauty and joy! When we use these functions in human consciousness for communication, there is no possibility of misunderstanding! There is no lack of communication! When you "speak" the language of love, without words and logic, you are able to share you very "being" with

131

the other person. Everything becomes clear and there are never any misunderstandings in this kind of communication. We all have heard of "communication" through love and intuition. When we have love .... we are able to have "true" communication because in true love the ability to "identify" one's self with the other person is triggered. When one completely identifies himself with the other person, communication takes place through the "transference" of the conscious experience! So much so that, when one is "in love", one begins to "automatically" do things whch the other person himself would have done! One begins to "feel" the same way as the beloved would feel! In the experience of love, the "lover" disappears and the "beloved" alone remains! And the experience and feelings of the beloved become the experience and feelings of both! Human communication, then, is best achieved through the process of love. Unfortunately, one finds very little love of this high order in this world. Most of the time when we talk of love, we are talking of attachments. These attachments are not the same thing as love. There is a basic difference between attachment and love. In attachment there is the consciousness and awareness of two. In love, the awareness of "two" disappears and only the awareness of "one" remains! If somebody says to you "I love you", you can be sure that this is a case of attachment! In the awareness of that person both the "I" and the "YOU" prevail. The person is conscious and aware of both "I" and "YOU".

If you look deeply into this, you will discover that such a person is more in love with the "I" than the "you"! It will turn out to be just another big "ego trip" which he calls love. If his "I" is hurt in any way, then this "I love you" will instantly become "I hate you"! This immediate transformation of "I love you" into "I hate you" occurs because there was no "love" in the first place! It was mere attachment. It

132

was self-interest; selfish attachment. When a person is really in love, he will be so much filled with "you" that he will have no time to notice the "I" or the love! When I visualize a person in love, I visualize such a person saying "you, you, you"! He has no time to think of the "I", nor of the love that he is experiencing! He has filled his awareness so much with "you", that he has nothing else left in it except you! Love is the art, the practice, the science, the ability to "completely" identify one's self with the other. It is the experience of "togetherness" and "oneness"! Not oneness in the physical sense, but oneness in the sense of experience! It is oneness in the spirit! It is oneness at every level of awareness! When that feeling of oneness is there, then even the physical separation of those in love does not really matter! The oneness persists and they "stay" together in that awareness. Even when physically apart, the love exists.

In "true" love, there is no possessiveness. You will not feel that the object of love, the beloved, is being taken away, because no one can take away true love! Real human communication can happen only through this kind of love and not through words and attachment. Therefore, there is a possibility of overcoming the limitations and inadequacy of language by using that part of human awareness which is not based upon the use of the mind. But, when we examine real life situations, we find that there is yet another process, which causes misunderstanding and conflict in our personal relationships and which has not been fully understood, namely, the "karmic" process.

Very often, we do not know why we communicate with people in a particular way. When two people meet, there is no reason for them to fight, yet they fight! There is no reason for them to disagree, yet they disagree! There is no reason for them to hate each other, yet they hate each other.

There is no reason for them to love each other, yet they love each other! There is no reason for them to have such intense affection for each other, yet they have it. If everything was based entirely upon what we were saying or doing, then these things would not happen. But they do happen and very often they interfere with communication between human beings. The real reason for this is that our mind does not react to a person "independently". It reacts with a "karmic load"; a load of previous impressions that it carries! Now, for those who believe in "reincarnation" it is easy to understand this. But, for those who do not, it is a little difficult to understand what this "load of karma" is that each person carries with him.

If one can understand the law of karma, it becomes easier to understand how this karmic load affects the process of communication between two people. The karmic load is the load of "samskara" or attitudes and modes which we carry with us from previous experiences with the same people in past lives! There is sufficient evidence, that only reincarnation could have created certain attitudes that we have in this life based upon previous experiences in a former life! Very often, when you meet a person, and you like him, it is because of the "continuation" of love from a past life! And when you hate a person, whom you have just met, for no reason, it is because of "something" that had happened in the past life, and you are merely reacting to a past experience! Very often people ask, "Why don't we remember our past lives?" Actually, we have never forgotten our past lives. The thing is, we only remember our past impressions but we don't remember the "events" of the past lives! We have forgotten the events, but we have remembered the "lessons" of these events. And, we carry these lessons that we have learned from past lives within the mind. We remember them! We never forget them! When we meet a new situation or a new

134

person, the old impacts and the old impressions are still with us. These impressions are carried in the human mind but they are NOT carried by the human soul! They are "transferred" from one body to another body through the human mind! The mind alone carries these impressions. There is no Karma except in the human mind.

I want to clarify this because people think that Karma is a physical thing. It has nothing to do with the body. Karma, or these impressions which are carried from life to life, are only carried by the human mind! But when the mind uses a body, it transfers the effect of these impressions to the body. When the mind goes into a new body, it makes the body act in the same way as it would have if it were the same body! The action and reaction is in the mind, but it is followed by an action and reaction in the body. Suppose the human mind is unaware of what is going on but something happens to the body, then no Karma is involved at all! The body can neither have Karma, nor create new Karma, nor work out any past Karma! Only the mind can create Karma! Only the mind can "pay back" any Karma. Karma is only connected with the mind. Therefore, the mind brings this limitation along with it when used for communicating with other human beings. This is a very major limitation.

I do not believe that it has to be taken for granted that there is a "law of Karma". I do not suggest that you simply believe that there is such a thing as Karma. If anyone wants to investigate or verify whether such a thing exists or not, I suggest that you simply examine your own mind! You do not have to look anywhere else. The laboratory is in your head where your mind is situated. Just take a look at your own mind! If you become an observer of your own mind, you will clearly see what "karmic samskars", what impressions your mind is carrying! You can easily see this load of Karma on the mind when you become an observer of your own thoughts!

Thoughts are simply a stream of "words" passing through the mind! These words move through the mind all the time whether we are awake or asleep; whether we are talking or we are quiet; whether we are walking or lying down! The mind never stops thinking in words! Even when the mind visualizes an image, it must comment upon that image with words! Even if the mind wants to perceive something, it can only perceive it by repeating to itself what is being seen! The mind is constantly talking and constantly listening! The mind does not understand anything unless it speaks and listens to what it has said! All sense perceptions are converted by the mind through this process of listening. If you merely see a thing, and don't allow the mind to "interpret" what you have seen, you will not see anything! The interpretative function of the mind is performed by the device of "listening". The mind interprets perception by "recording", in words, what it has seen, felt, touched, smelt or tasted! All sense perceptions are reduced to one "single" 'perception of listening! That is why it is said that the mind has ears, perhaps eyes—but no other senses!

The mind, basically, has only the sense of listening. Through listening it converts words into meanings. When this mind is used for communication between two human beings, it creates all kinds of problems. The mind, by its very nature, can only use the "intellect" for communication. Intellect is the power to analyze. Analysis means the "breaking up" of a thing into pieces. When it breaks something, it creates violence and tension!

The mind has the capacity to break people's lives; to break people's hearts; to break people's love; to "crack" itself

136

up! This terrible destructive power of the mind arises out of its very nature. And when the mind is used for communication, it creates all of these problems. It creates doubts and fears all the time! The mind is constantly creating suspicion and doubt; even in the case of the experience of love. When the mind steps in, it breaks the lovers apart! It creates suspicion, misunderstanding and, ultimately, a divorce! The more we rely on the mind, the more we suffer. The mind converts the beautiful experience of love into the ugly experience of attachment and separation. The mind gives us the feeling of separation.

So, communication with the mind creates all the problems that exist in our human relationships. When people try to "think" and communicate, they always run into difficulties. The beautiful human experiences that come to people are destroyed by thinking! On the other hand, the "intuitive faculty" of the soul gives "instant" knowledge about a certain event, about a certain person! It is so beautiful that we accept it and rejoice in that knowledge intuitively. We can have the true communication without limitations, without problems, only if we communicate with the soul! Only when we are able to have "oneness" in experience can we have "real" communication!

XV

LONELY, ALONE

LONELINESS is a very commonly used word, but its causes have not been discussed as often. We are lonely because we do not know how to communicate. Even in the midst of a crowd, we remain lonely if there is no communication with another person. On the other hand, if we know how to communicate — even without words — we are never lonely! When we feel that we are not understood, this feeling of loneliness, this "unexpressed" feeling of loneliness, grows. And, loneliness will continue to grow until we can communicate with people! Loneliness implies that you are still seeking the "other". Loneliness means that you have missed the experience of love and have simply fallen into a dark and dismal state of despair. Loneliness means that you have become afraid, frightened .... withdrawn. Indeed, far more people die of loneliness than from any physical illness. More people have been driven totally insane because of this loneliness than by any other kind of misfortune! The world is full of lonely people, and because of their loneliness, they go on creating more and more ways to escape from it. This loneliness is so painful, so ugly and death-like, that every possible means to escape from it has been devised. Alcohol, drugs, sex clubs, etc., have become the mainstay for millions of people! Entertainment, of all types, has become the biggest and the fastest growing market in every society! The lonely person will sit glued to his TV for five or six hours a day in search of anything that will help dilute his state of loneliness! What else can he do? Where to go? With whom can he communicate? No one "understands" him. His wife, his children, his family .... no one seems to understand. So what else is there left to do? He cannot "talk" to anyone. But when we learn to communicate with people through means other than words, we need not be lonely. People no longer "talk" to each other. At the most they talk "at" each other, but never to each other! They have completely forgotten how to touch, how to "reach" each other. They have become like the tracks of a railway — running very close to each other, in the same direction — but never meeting! Husbands and wives, teachers and students, even many so-called lovers, are simply moving in the same direction, meeting nowhere! Running very close to each other, hoping that some day and somehow they will meet but this is just a hope! It is an illusion! The railway tracks "appear" to meet in the distance, but they never meet! Similarly, people never "meet" in spite of their best efforts. Neither do they ever "really" understand what the other is talking about! The husband is trapped in his own loneliness and the wife is trapped in her own loneliness. A husband and a wife are two people living together and yet both are very lonely. It is the saddest thing to see in the world.

You are lonely because nobody understands you and you don't understand anybody! You are lonely because the only way you know how to communicate is through words, and words mean different things to us. You are lonely because you don't understand what the other person's words mean. You are also lonely because you don't know your self! It is interesting to note that people do not know how to keep even their own company!

"Aloneness" is totally different from loneliness. Aloneness is the simple joy of just being with yourself. The joy of being in your "own space". But only those who "know thyself" . . . . who know who they are, what they are and why they are, will have the courage to be alone! For them, aloneness is beautiful, it is a blessing. Just to be alone with one's own self is ecstasy! But, we have lost this capacity to have ourselves as company. The reason is that we are no longer within ourselves! If this body or cage containing our human consciousness and awareness; this head of ours which contains the brain and soul and everything — the living force — if this is regarded to be our house, how long do we stay there?

You would be surprised to note that we spend our entire life wandering outside! We never come home! We are in everybody else's house, entangled in other people's problems! Through the process of divided and scattered attention, we occupy every other place except our own home! And who occupies our home? Thoughts, negative thoughts! They are our tenants! We who are supposed to live in our house have leased it out to negative thoughts! Why don't we come back and stay in our own homes and enjoy ourselves? If we were at home, we would at least be able to enjoy our own company! But by always being outside and not being able to communicate with anybody, we simply remain lonely. This feeling of loneliness persists because we have lost the capacity to enjoy our own company! Even if we have no communication with anyone; even if we do not know what love is, we can still avoid loneliness if we know how to be with ourselves. But this capacity to come back and be with ourselves has also been lost and instead we have identified ourselves with things which are not ourselves!

We have not identified ourselves with our "conscious self". We have identified ourselves with the body in which we are housed. Therefore, it becomes impossible to have the com-

140

pany of ourselves! If I think that this body is 'me', then I must seek company outside it, and since outside this body I cannot communicate, I become lonely! We can easily remove loneliness if we know how to relax inside her own selves. The biggest problem people face is the inability to relax "within" themselves. Mental yoga, where you sit calmly, quietly and concentrate within yourself, is a very good device to remove loneliness. What do you do in yoga? You have union with yourself! You pull your thoughts and your attention back to the place where you belong; and once there, you simply relax and watch the great drama which is taking place outside your body! One of the main reasons why we are so tense, and why loneliness becomes so over-powering and so difficult to bear, is because we do not look at the drama of life in its proper perspective. We take it far too seriously!

If we watch the drama of life while sitting in our cushioned chair behind the eyes, we will remain very happy and never become lonely. When we go and watch a movie and sit in the audience and watch the screen, the whole thing looks real. It looks so real that sometimes it can make us cry! When the characters laugh, we laugh! When there is a tragic event, we feel sad! It affects us! But we have never seen anyone from the audience running up to prevent a murder that is about to take place on the screen! This is because we all know that it just a drama. Even though the drama involves and affects us, and even though our consciousness is part of the drama, we do not rush up from our chairs! We know, at the back of our minds, that it is just a play! But here, in this four-dimensional, five-dimensional screen portraying the drama of life, we jump up and try to prevent that which cannot be prevented, instead of sitting back and enjoying it!

And, this is what makes us more lonely, because then we discover that we are helpless . . . we can do nothing!

141

And, disappointment is a great creator of loneliness. When we expect something to happen, and it does not happen, we feel lonely. When our expectations are not fulfilled, and we think we have been "abandoned", then we become lonely. When we are let down by a friend, we feel lonely. The rest of the world may be with us, but our attention gets rivetted to this one event. When we are disappointed, we feel that the whole world has been cut off from us! For that moment, this experience of snapping ties with one individual pushes us into complete depression, solitude and loneliness! It's strange that when someone has 10 friends, and only one disappoints him, he feels lonely. The other nine cannot comfort him because he feels that the whole world has been lost. He never expected this. When a man says, "I never expected this", he feels disappointed! Why should all of these feelings of disappointment and loneliness come to us in the first place? What is the nature of this loneliness? Why are we lonely? There must be some good reason.

The reason which the mystics and spiritual teachers give is quite amazing. They say that, like love, loneliness is also natural to us! Man feels lonely, because man basically is alone! You are born alone and you will die alone! But in between your birth and death, you try to be a part of someone or something else. However, this is impossible! Your "aloneness" will still remain. Modern man is becoming more aware of his loneliness simply because today he has more time to "think". Technology has given him more time to pause and see his real situation. In the past, the struggle to survive, to make a living, was so time consuming that man had no time to think! But today, because of the affluence of our society, the real problems of life have started to surface! When the ordinary necessities of life have been ulfilled, only then do we become conscious of the feeling of "deep" loneliness. Then alone does one become aware that "he is

142

lonely", even in the midst of affluence and other people . . . he is still somehow by himself alone! And "love" is simply a device to overcome the experience of this loneliness! But, loneliness is as "natural" to us as love. And the explanation that the mystics give us is that this is due to the fact that the creator of all of us was only "one" . . . . alone! He had no colleague; no mate; no partner; no friend! There was no other being, no other God except God!

Since there was only one God, one creator, one consciousness, one total consciousness, one experiencer, he, she, it, whatever it was . . . it was lonely! In fact, this is also the reason given in Genesis, for creation! The explanation given for creation is the "loneliness" of God. A lot of people feel that if we have to go through so much trouble in order to go back to God, to realize him, why did he push us out of his home and send us into this world in the first place? Why should He have created this miserable place and then proceed to call us back from here, "find me", "come to me" . . . Why? Wasn't he happy there with us already? The answer is no! When there was no creation there was no "you" . . . God was lonely! Thus the "entire" creation was simply an experience for God! Man has been made in the image of God and carries within him not only the creative power of God, but also the "loneliness" of God! Man, in his inmost self, realizes that there is only one. And this ultimate realization is the "realization of loneliness". But just as God has created a world so real that it looks as real as Himself, likewise, man has created an experience of "love" and "togetherness" which is as real as himself! Hence, both God and man have removed their loneliness! Loneliness, then, is the basic experience of both God and man.

The creator has always had a creation in order not to be lonely. And we have always had the capacity to love in order not to be lonely. We have regenerated the experiences through the mental process of being separated, being isolated, and of being lonely. The answer to the problem of loneliness, then, is to stop thinking and start loving! Stop using the mind for everything, especially in human relations. Use it where it belongs. Use it for studying a book, use it for science, use it for technology, use it for other educational purposes, but don't use it in human relations! Use the intuitive processes and love for dealing with human beings. And, you will never feel lonely.

XVI

WHAT IS LOVE AND MARRIAGE?

THIS is a subject of great interest in the whole wide world, whether in the East or in the West. Matrimony has dominated the field of our social sciences right from the very beginning of society. At one time, it was believed that all marriages were "made" in heaven. In some societies they still believe this, but they don't believe that there is any heaven left! The fact that marriages are "made" on Earth has finally dawned upon people today. But still, there are some people who are not even sure if marriages are made at all!

I am reminded of an experience I had when my wife and I first visited this country, the United States, in 1962. We were invited by a friend in Washington D.C. to a party to meet a newly-wed young couple. We were told that we would be delighted to meet such a loving couple, just married six months ago. So, we met the couple at the party. They were not as young as we had thought, but they looked very happily married. As they walked in, everybody congratulated them and so did we. Along with them was a six-year-old boy. We were told that this boy was the lady's son. My wife couldn't understand how a couple married six months earlier could have a son six years old! So she whispered in my ear and asked, "How are marriages done in this country?" I said, "I don't know, why don't you ask these people?" So she asked the lady, newly married, "How come you have a son who is so big?" She said, "Oh, he is from my previous husband!" My wife was shocked! She wondered how it was possible—at all—for a woman to "love" anybody else when she had already loved somebody earlier but had separated. How was it possible to have the experience of love thereafter? According to her, it was not possible. Therefore, when the people around us were telling us that this is a very lovey-dovey couple, they were referring to something very superficial, and not what we call love... what we understand as "love". Later on, of course, I told my wife that you should find out from them how they managed to love each other even though they were married previously. So my wife took the opportunity of asking the lady, "Since you have been married earlier, and you have loved and have slept with a man before, how can you possibly love this man the same way?" And the lady said, "Oh, that's no problem because he's not my second husband, he's my fourth husband! I'm his fifth wife! So we can love each other!" This complicated the issue even more.

There was another incident, involving a psychiatrist and his wife, whom I knew. They seemed a very happy couple when I first met with them. Several years later, I came to the United States again. They invited me to stay with them. The doctor told me with great joy, "Ishwar, do you know Alice and I have separated?" I was surprised that this was "good news" he was giving me! I asked him why he was so happy. He said, "I'm happy because now we are no longer married and can now live together!" The point that he was making was that all the problems that had arisen between them in their marriage had been solved, and they could now live together as two human beings!

There is yet another interesting episode I remember. A couple, Charles and Emily, whom I knew for many years,

146

loved each other dearly. They could not love anyone else! But the moment they got married, they started to fight with each other until, finally, they got divorced! But the moment they were divorced, they started to love each other again! Then, they married again! They married each other three times! They never married anyone else! Theirs was a very unusual case.

All these instances illustrate that even between people, who love each other, problems arise only if they try to love each other "because" of marriage! I have seen a lot of people, men and women, who say they have great love for each other! But the moment they get married that "love" disappears. Social scientists have been examining this problem both in the East and in the West. And I'm aware that they have come to a universal conclusion as to what is responsible for the break-up of so many marriages. Even if the marriage began with a great expressed love between those who got married, they have found out that after marriage, the man and woman took each other for granted! And the human mind does not want to be taken for granted! This is the basic problem in marriage! In marriage, the problem is that the wife feels she is no longer "cared for" as she was before she was married! The husband feels the wife is no longer as "interested in him" as she was before he was married! They take each other for granted and the "old relationship" is destroyed! The beauty of the period of courtship and wooing, of meeting and dating, is destroyed by marriage. How, then, can such a marriage be long lasting? And, this goes on happening again and again.

You fall in love with someone, marry him or her, and soon thereafter love simply disappears! You never pay any "attention" to the other person . . . the other person never pays any attention to you! You simply take each other for granted! You become too engrossed with your own needs, hence love disappears. Almost always, by the time the honeymoon is over—love is gone! Then, only two empty bodies remain! You can continue to have sex, mere physical contact, . . . but sexual contact alone can never be satisfying, fulfilling. Hence, a deep frustration arises, a death-like hopelessness and boredom grips you and the only way out now is to run; to escape . . . . to divorce!

This is a society where nobody gives each other any attention! If the husband wants to talk to the wife, he finds that she is always "too busy" with the children, the dishes, the housework and so on. And when the wife wants some attention from the husband, he is "too tired" from the job or must see the game on TV! In fact, the average American husband and wife talk to each other less than 30 minutes per day! And this, remember, is the average! And included in these 30 minutes are the nagging, fighting, complaining and everything else! Otherwise, in the remaining hours, no attention is paid to each other! Society has MESSED us up so much that everyone is on the verge of getting a divorce! All love has disappeared; all communication has been destroyed; all friendship is gone; no sensitivity remains!

In our society, we have not trained our minds to take care of the problem of ego; to take care of the problems that are created by taking each other for granted; to take care of the problems that come from expecting too much from somebody! We have not trained our minds for this. Therefore, what else can we expect, except a higher divorce rate?

This leads us to another very interesting point that is sometimes made. When people go from the West to the East, they are startled to find that a large number of people get married without having met their spouses before! We find that these so-called "arranged marriages" seem to last longer than the so-called "love" marriages arising out of dating and wooing each other! Looks funny, but it is true! Why should this happen? You will find that the answer is simple! In the case of an arranged marriage, the two parties never had a chance to know each other! They never had a chance to "shift" the experience from one of love to that of being taken for granted! They only had one experience, the experience of matrimony. The closeness which arises between two lovers in Western society before marriage, and which ends abruptly with marriage, begins to develop only AFTER marriage in the Eastern society! The honeymoon is the BEGINNING of a great love affair. Love doesn't end with the honeymoon! In fact, it only starts AFTER the honeymoon is over! It is a totally different phenomenon! Intimacy and love go on growing! A great reverence for each other is ultimately developed. And, therefore, in Eastern societies, marriages last longer!

Even in these societies, we are being constantly prodded by the West to come out of our primitiveness; to join the "modern" mainstream of social life, where marriages are taking place because of this so-called love! But, the divorce rate in the West is going up! Today, we find that the maximum number of divorces are taking place amongst those couples who have married after dating! Not amongst those who married without dating! What is the problem? Why should marriage destroy the love that existed between two people? "Being taken for granted", what does this mean?

It simply means that before marriage, we were trying to put on our best appearance. We created a "false image" of ourselves to impress the other! We did it for the sake of our ego; to satisfy our inflated ego! To prove that we were "better" than what we actually are! We do all this, in order to get married! And once we are married, it is no longer necessary to keep this "charming" and "false" image up! The image is thrown down and the reality is discovered! Each person sees the other's "reality", becomes disappointed and gets divorced! If you look closely at this problem, you will find that it is really one of human ego! If there were no ego, there would be no divorce! We always want to assert that we are right and the other person is wrong . . . always! Good, bad, right, wrong, moral, immoral . . . These are our own ideas! And, we are always trying to impose our ideas on the other person! Try to understand this point. You are always trying to "decide" what the other person should do . . . must do! What is right, what is wrong. But whatsoever you decide CANNOT be right, because it is YOUR choice—not the other person's choice! The "chooser" is always you! The chooser is the ego! This ego always poisons other people; always pollutes the other person's existence! Therefore, even if you "think" you are right, automatically you will be wrong! Who are you to make other people's choices? In a small group, I once recommended a very interesting experiment. I said, "Why don't you practise an experiment of saying that the other person is always right! Just see if any of your marriages will break up if you can "artificially" practise saying that the other person is right!" You'll be surprised to know that none of the marriages has yet broken up! Thus, we have been able to place our finger on the real cause of the breaking up of marriages. It is ego. "I am right, everyone else is wrong!" "I know better than anyone else!" This is precisely what is happening in every area of human relationship, not just matrimony.

Surprisingly enough, people continuously talk of developing the soul; of going to "higher levels" of consciousness; of becoming perfect; of achieving great development in civilization and moving towards perfection. We talk of these high things, not realizing that these high achievements are not possible so long as we have not tackled the problem of the human ego! This feeling that "I'm right and the other person is wrong", this feeling must cease! If it does not stop, you cannot solve the problems and conflicts in human relations. In modern societies, we simply go on increasing the ego of people, not reducing it. When the ego is satisfied, we feel happy for the time being, but our human relationship is destroyed. So many other things are also destroyed in the process, but we don't seem to care; we don't seem to "link" the two things, together. If we really want to solve our basic social problems, divorce being one of them, we have to first solve the problem of ego. How do we do this?

There are many approaches to solving the problem of the human ego. One is to weaken it, by always saying, "I'am nobody, everyone else is the greatest!" Instead of saying, "I'am always right", say "I am wrong, others may be right"! Instead of saying, "all this is mine", say "I don't have anything; it belongs to others!" Instead of saying, "I know everything; I can teach everyone" say "I know nothing; anyone can teach me!" This is the approach by which the ego is "weakened" and the problems arising out of a strong ego are, to some extent, minimized. But this is a dangerous method, because after a while (when the ego is weakened too much) the capacity to carry on the experiment is also destroyed! You have weakened the ego in order to solve the problem of ego, and if the ego itself is weakened . . . who will solve the problem? What will you be able to do after that? Therefore, for controlling the ego, it is found that weakening it is not the best solution to the problem. The solution is not to weaken the ego; not to MAKE yourself humble. This is simply turning the ego upside down, a headstand . . . standing on your head instead of your feet. But still, you will remain in the same spot! No "growth" has really taken place! On the other hand,

151

you can take the opposite approach by simply removing the "individuation" from ego, the individual aspect of ego. "We are all great"! Not that only "I am great" but that "we are all great!" Instead of saying this is "my" house, say "this is 'our' house"! Instead of saying "this is *my* job not yours", say "this is 'our' job to do"!

With spiritual discipline, one can train one's mind to such an extent that one can say "nothing is mine and that everything is God's!" In this case we are weakening the ego. Or, we can say "everything is mine because I'am 'one' with God!" It has been discovered that when you "expand" the ego to cover totality, the problem of ego disappears without weakening the ego! Therefore, what really creates the problem is not ego per se, but that part of ego which "separates" you from the rest, the individuating part of ego! When we take care of this, by talking in terms of "we" rather than "I", then we are able to solve the problem of the ego! And if we apply this rule in life, we discover that the relationship between a man and a woman will change immediately and immensely! If men and women live in terms of "we" and not in terms of "I", the divorce rate will go down.

After analyzing this problem from this aspect, we find that ego is our only problem. Ego has to be taken care of. And, it cannot be taken care of by beating it down! It can be taken care of only by "expanding" it to totality. When this is done, the acute social problem of divorce disappears!

XVII

THE UNION OF MAN AND WOMAN

OUR subject is the male and female principle, not "man" and "woman". It just so happens that men and women are also male and female, but this subject is much wider in scope, and has a much greater significance, than merely a discussion of the man-woman relationship. All women do not necessarily represent the female principle. When I speak of the female principle, I mean the "receptive"; that which "surrenders"; which is like a "womb", that which is open, . . . "passive". Half of humanity will be of this type, "feminine". But, the other half will be totally opposite. The male principle represents that which is "aggressive"; which is "active"; that which seeks to "penetrate" . . . to make "effort". The other half of humanity is "masculine". The male-female principle is not only expressed at this level of reality, but it exists throughout every level of creation.

In fact, the basis of all human experience lies in a higher plane of consciousness. This existence around us is merely a "copy" of existence at the higher levels. It is a sort of reflection of what is going on there. This means that, if the male and female relationship is of special significance here, it must be of special significance at the higher levels also. I am stating this at the outset, because many people believe that it is the relationship between man and woman at this

153

physical level that is responsible for all our marital problems. It is commonly believed that once we leave this world, this relationship will be over! It is not so. This relationship continues even at higher levels of consciousness! Therefore, let me begin by saying that the entire process of creation, the entire experience at the physical level, is based upon the male and female principle! Nothing can be experienced which does not fall into this classification of male and female. You may call it male and female; you may call it positive and negative; you may call it "pairs of opposites", but no experience is possible for a human being at the physical plane of consciousness without "experiencing" it through this duality.

If you examine each aspect of the experiences that you have, you will discover that each one is dependent upon its opposite! Sex, that is . . . "coupling"—the act of two opposites joining together to manufacture a single event— exists in everything we experience! In every case, whenever there is a "polarity" there is "sex" . . . the opposites become attracted! This has always been happening and it will go on happening. It is happening because of the male and female principle which shapes and determines the nature of all human, as well as non-human, phenomena at this level of reality! The male and female principle governs every activity, whether animate or inanimate! Look at anything that has been created in this universe, and you will see that it is based upon this principle of the positive and negative; based upon the principle of male and female. Even atoms and molecules are constructed on this basis; matter is created from the building blocks of the male and female, and every living thing is created via the male and female principle!

We experience this world in a very limited framework, the framework of time, space, and causation. A frame in

154

which nothing can happen if there is no "time" for it to happen; a frame in which space is needed where something can happen; a frame in which all things that happen must have a cause-and-effect relationship. And, in order to have these things, you must have the opposite of everything! Therefore, the very essence of human experience is based on the male and female principle.

When we look at it from the spiritual angle, we find that it has great symbolic significance. The male and female principle is given great symbolic significance because it is the relationship between the creator and creation! It is the relationship between the "purusha" and "prakriti". It is the relationship between the "sought" and the "seeker". In this relationship, the "sought" is the male principle and the "seeker" is the female principle. In fact, the word "yoga", which is used to connote the quest for God-realization, means "union". And what is this union other than the union of these two principles? Therefore, you will discover that, from whatever angle you look at this male-female principle, the union of male and female is the "culmination" of all seeking! If the culmination of all achievement is the union of male and female, then it follows that the disruption of the union is caused by "breaking" it up into male and female parts! The fact of the matter is that all life has been split up into male and female from that state in which there is no male or female! A level where there is no time, no space, no law of cause and effect! This state, where there is no time, space and causation, is the state beyond the mind! The human mind cannot function except within this framework! Therefore, human awareness, when it transcends the mind, can have the experience of a state in which there is no male-female principle, no separation, but only union. Until one can transcend the boundaries of the mind, one has to contend with this male-female principle and with all the problems

155

that arise from it. The common belief is that the male and female principle is a very mechanical, very "impersonal" principle until it comes to the human level. And when it reaches the human level, it "suddenly" becomes a very personal principle and there is a great necessity for the "right male" to meet the "right female". But, one does not know who the right partner is! And people are continuously searching for what they call their "soul mates"!

The "soul mates" that people are trying to find are their mates from the "original" union from which they were split up! Suppose I have a large number of plates, say, a hundred plates on the table for party, for a dinner, and by chance I push them and they fall down and all get broken into pieces. Then I try to quickly assemble them and put them back together . . . try to repair them. But I find that I can't put them together "perfectly", because the cracks are not exactly in the same places! However, if I find two pieces of the same plate, the cracks join up fine and I can't even see where it was broken! But, if the pieces are from two different plates, although they look similar, when I try to join them there will be gaps between them!

Similarly, the male and female portions of the soul are going around searching for their lost counterparts, and this desire to "find" the other part drives people into this whole business of marriage, attraction, attachments and so on! Most of the male|female relationships are based on this kind of frantic activity. It is almost impossible to find two people who happen to be two parts of the same broken plate! However, if they meet, they instantly fit with each other and are, therefore, sometimes referred to as "soul mates"; as mates who "broke off" from one soul, which existed beyond the region of the mind. When the soul comes within the region of the mind, to have experience through the framework of

156

time, space, and causation, this search for the other part continues.

It is a "symbolic search"; a search of the soul for its "totality"; the search of the "individual" for the "whole"; the search of man for God! This symbolic search goes on, but as human beings, we always make a mistake. We misinterpret the symbols and give them some other meanings. We have misinterpreted many symbols given to us. The desire of the female sex and the male sex to have union, which is supposed to be symbolic of the desire of a human being to meet God, is misinterpreted to such an extent that it is even condemned as something unholy and undesirable! The result is, the symbolic "value" of this union is lost!

But, how do we find the right soul mate? Should we go on following the system of divorce by which a person keeps on rotating from one mate to another? More likely than not, the person will still reach the wrong soul mate; will still make the wrong choice and soon discover that there still remains a gap! Then again, an attempt is made to continue searching! And this is not just a one-lifetime affair, it is repeated — again and again. It goes on lifetime after lifetime. This effort of trying to find the right counterpart goes on for ever! Sometimes the question has been asked, "Supposing there is one plate left on the shelf that did not fall and is not broken, and also suppose we are able to find the exact parts of a broken plate, the soul mates, and put them together. Then the question arises as to which plate is better? What is the difference? The answer, surprisingly enough, is that the one that broke and was rejoined perfectly is better than the one that never broke! The plate that never broke is simply a plate with no other added experience except that it is a plate. The second plate, however, having been joined to perfection, has the "added" experience of having known what it is to be separated and what it is to be joined! Therefore, the second plate has gone through an experience which we call the "experience of love"; of union; of joining! That is why it is said that, even though souls may exist in timelessness; in the house of truth; with the Lord Himself; they are not as lucky as the ones that have had the opportunity of becoming males or females! Having come to this world, they have had the added opportunity to experience separation and then again become one with the Lord! To experience union .... to experience Love! In fact, we distinguish between these souls by calling them "HANS", birds which have been turned into swans from crows.

Therefore, it is considered that this human life, in which it is possible to have this kind of transformation — where the male and female principle is symbolically used to rise to higher levels of consciousness — is the highest level of human development! Even though there are higher levels in consciousness which are more beautiful in terms of experience, they lack the opportunity and possibility of providing the experience of the seeker and the sought! That is why, the human being has been considered to be "HIGHER" than even the "gods in the heavens"! The reason is because the gods in the heavens know everything that is going to happen! They know whether they will be there or not be there. They know what is going to happen tomorrow, therefore they have no free will. They are living in a state of great knowledge and bliss, but with no free will! Therefore, they can never become a "seeker" and look for the sought.

On the other hand, the human being, denied that knowledge and given the "illusion" of free will, can, through the use of this free will, become a seeker. It gives him a unique opportunity to have the experience of being the seeker and the sought, and have the fulfilment of union. This is why the human being has been called the "highest" form of creation next to the Lord Himself. It is also sometimes said that the human being is made in the "image of God". The reason that this statement is made is because the human being and God alone have the "experience" of free will! Nobody else has it. Throughout this creation, from the physical and lowest level of a human being, to the highest level of the ultimate creator or total consciousness, we find that everything is known! There is no free will! The ultimate creator alone has the experience of free will, because He has created! And a human being has the experience of free will because he does not "know" what is going to happen! Therefore, these states of "freedom" are the two highest states of consciousness! The human being is a very important soul in the creation, even more important than those who live in heaven, the angels! In fact, those who can travel in the astral regions and have the opportunity to see what goes on in the heavens above, will discover that the angels are trying their best to come down to the level of the human being so that they can become "seekers" in order to have union with God!

Sometimes, people have the feeling that in their past life, they had a higher level of awareness and had reached a plane of consciousness higher than the present level. Why, if this is true, have they come down? Is this spiritual progress or not? It is progress! Because, having already risen to a certain level of consciousness from where they could rise no further, they had to come down to a level where they could experience the "illusion" of free will and become seekers again in order to make further progress! It is as if you bend down in order to take a big leap upwards! Therefore, it is not strange for some souls to come down from a higher level of awareness to a lower level! We have discussed a great deal about the male and female principle from the spiritual point of view, but even if you look at it from the point of view of physical science you will discover that all matter is based upon this same principle! The electrons and the protons amalgamate, and their union — the collapsing of the negative into the positive and the formation of matter or dense energy — is based upon these pairs of opposites! And now, with the discovery of "anti-matter" you will find that the pairs of opposites are maintained even by this totally different type of matter! You might not have heard of the "quasars" which have been observed at the fringes of space.

Einsteinian physics has taught us that we can "know", but cannot travel at a velocity greater than the velocity of light. In fact, Einstein believed that the highest velocity was the velocity of light! Human locomotion, or any kind of locomotion of matter, must therefore be confined to speeds and velocities approximating the velocity of light. But when these quasars were discovered, billions of light years away, to be moving at velocities higher than the velocity of light, the question came up, "How do we explain the movement of physical matter way out in space that is travelling at velocities higher than the velocity of light?" The calculations revealed that these particles of matter were moving at immense velocities — far greater than the velocity of light! They may sometimes slow down, but will never slow down to the velocity of light. Their speed is the "opposite" of light! Therefore, they are a kind of anti-matter moving at an "anti-velocity" of light!

The more we discover about these truths from the physical sciences, the more we find that they are based upon the pairs of opposites! We find that we would see no light if there was no darkness! Suppose that light was such a thing that you could see it, whether you opened your eyes or closed them; whether you were awake or asleep. If light were to be seen by us at all times, do you know we would never notice that light! We would not even experience it, because it would be there all the time! What is "there" all the time cannot be experienced by us; only that which has an "opposite" can create an experience for us! There are very few things we would even notice unless their opposites were also "there".

This world is called an illusion, "maya", because everything is dependent upon the pairs of opposites and these opposites keep on changing! That, which is "really" there all the time, would not ever change! It would not be an illusion. The only thing in the world which is not an illusion, which we know is always there and, therefore, is never noticed by us, is "consciousness"! It is "consciousness" that creates the world, but since it is always there and has no opposite, we do not notice it; we do not see it! Everything else is experienced by consciousness on the basis of the pairs of opposites!

Sometimes people ask, "If God is good; if the Creator is merciful; then why did He create so much misery upon this earth? Why did He create darkness? Why did He create evil? Why did He create ignorance?" The point is, that if He did not create these things, how would we experience joy, goodness, light and knowledge? Would there be any meaning for these experiences if their opposites were not there? If you look at the "totality" of an experience, you will find that its opposite is as necessary as the event itself! Therefore, this so called "negative side" of life has been created in order to experience the "positive" side of life! The role that is played by the two sides can be best understood if we see the picture in its totality. When life is experienced in totality, it is very beautiful and perfect! In fact, nobody can improve it! You discover the perfection in this creation only when you see the totality of creation all at once! Now, this ability

161

to see the creation "all at once" is achieved by transcending the mind! The break-up of one soul into male and female, the break-up of totality into the seeker and the sought, has been created in order to have a higher experience of becoming "one" through the experience of being two! And where is the dividing line? Where does the "one" become two and then become "one" again? What is the "wall" between the two, male and female, and the "one" .... the "union" of the two? What is this wall that has to be crossed? This wall is the wall of the human mind expressed in the form of ego!

XVIII

THE EGO

WHEN a human being says, "I'am saying this but you are saying that", the wall is being built up! When a human being says, "This is mine and that is yours", the wall is being built up. When the human being creates a "distinction" between his "self" and any other "self", the wall of ego is being built up. In reality, no one is different. When the "ego" is dropped, you will discover that everyone is the same! You are not exceptional! If you think that you are somehow exceptional, you must know very clearly that this is how everyone is feeling. To realize that one is "ordinary" is the most "extraordinary" thing in the world! Everyone is just like everyone else. The same emotions, the same desires that rule your life are present in everybody else.

But the ego creates a double-standard, one standard for itself and another one for everyone else. Whatsoever "you" think and feel is RIGHT, what "others" think is WRONG! This is why life has become such a mess; so full of misery, pain and frustration. You think that "you" are good and "everyone" else is bad. You feel that the whole world needs changing, . . . except you! But there is nothing wrong with the world; something is wrong with you! The problem is how to change yourself. The mind alone creates this wall of ego and is the only barrier. It is a big problem to cross this barrier because how can the mind cross its self? When we want to transcend the male-female separation, and the pain and agony that goes with that separation, to arrive at the union beyond this wall of ego, the mind gets in the way! If the mind is the thing that comes in the way, how can the "mind" take you beyond it? This is the biggest problem for those who want to overcome the problem of the ego. They do not "know" any other way of tackling this problem except by using the same mind! And how will the mind help them to demolish itself? How can they use the mind to demolish itself when it is the ego — the main part of the mind — which creates the wall?

This is the question which must be faced by all those who are serious and concerned about crossing this wall and moving into the state union, of love, rather than remaining in the state of separation. What do we do with our minds? Where is the solution to the problem posed by the mind? Do we have anything else to help us except the mind? Well, some people say let us leave the mind alone and resort to nature for the solution. Nature will give us the "message" that we need; the trees, the birds, the mountains, some little animals, perhaps a little lamb walking in the pasture will give us the answer! These are all God's "creatures". Therefore, if we want to find the answer, we can find it anywhere! When we look at nature, and feel the trees, the breeze and the mountains speaking to us, what is it that is really speaking? It is our own mind! There is nothing else that can give these words any meaning except our own mind! All animals, birds, and nature speak the language of the mind, and we remain where we were! And then we say, "Let us leave the animals and nature and go on to the books written by those realized souls who have transcended the mind. After all, the answers are already written in the scripture!" But, when you read a book, it means one thing today and tomorrow it will mean something entirely different! Why? The book is the same, the words are the same, but again it is the mind that is interpreting the words of the book. The mind, which is interpreting the words of the book, again comes in the way. Even when you turn to the world of ideas, and try and get some guidance from there you ultimately realize that this world of ideas is our own mind.

Therefore, in whatever direction we turn and wherever we go to find a way out of this problem of ego, it still turns out to be a way in which the guidance still comes from the mind itself. That is why a very large number of people seeking union, wanting to get away from this experience of birth and death, of time, space and causation, of male and female, of the pairs of opposites of the mind simply give up! Is there any solution which will take us beyond the realm of the mind? The only solution is to accept the mind of somebody else! But, why should one human being accept the dictates of the mind of another human being? If two human beings are equal, and if one human mind cannot solve its problems, how can the second human being, with his mind, solve those problems? If all human beings had "identical" minds, naturally they would not be able to solve each other's problems. But there is a little difference. Suppose you put a large number of radio receivers on a table, and removed the batteries or the electric cords from each of them so that none of them worked. Now they all look alike, but only when you put the battery in one of them will you hear the news of the world!

What is the difference between the radio receivers? They all look alike, they seem to be the same. The difference is that one has a "connection" with the power source and can give us the news of the world. The others don't have the connection! It is true that a man would normally refuse

165

to accept the advice of another man; would refuse to accept that another mind can guide him when his own mind cannot. However, if a man can be found who has a connection with the "power" that gives him the news of the world, he can then guide the others! Therefore, it is the man with the connection to a level of consciousness transcending the mind who alone can take us to the realm beyond the mind! If the person is merely a scholar, if he has simply read a lot and knows all the books of the world, he cannot help us! If he has all the book learning and all the wisdom of the world, he cannot take us up! The human being with the connection is not a "teacher", ... he is an "awakener" — a "liberator". If he simply lectures, debates, discusses — if he merely gives you "teachings" and "doctrines", he is of no help to you, he is merely a philosopher! He simply goes on increasing your accumulation of knowledge and information. He helps you to become "more" knowledgeable. He helps you to become more egotistical! But, if he has a connection through direct experience; by "personal" realization of the state of consciousness beyond the realm of the mind, then this human being becomes someone who can help you to get out of the dilemma of the mind! And then, you are able to cross this state of male and female principle and move into the state of union, into oneness! It is very difficult to say who that person is. When you look at twenty radio receivers, and one of them contains the battery, how will you know it? They all look alike! And with so many people claiming to have the "connection", plus our mind having the quality of creating doubts, uncertainties and distrust by its very nature, how will a seeker — a genuine seeker — recognize that human being who has the real connection? Can he apply any tests to find out if this is the guy who has transcended the region of the mind, and, therefore, can guide him? Is there any check list which he can apply? The fact of the matter is that he cannot! If a person had the ability to know who the man, with the "connection" beyond the mind, is, he would not need him! If that ability is already there, why would you need another person's help? You would not need any guide! But, if you cannot know who the guide is, then you need the guide! It means that you cannot find the guide; cannot locate a master, the "Guru", the one who has the connection; the one who can "transcend" the mind and help you transcend the mind and there is no way of finding him! So, what do you do? Must you remain in this state of helplessness? No, because even if you have no power to find the master, the master surely must have the power to find you! If such a man truly has a connection with that level of awareness, or consciousness, which is beyond the mind, surely he must know everything about you! And if he knows, then he should find you rather than you finding him. That is why it is said, "When the chela (disciple) is ready, the guru appears". We do not say, "When the disciple is ready he will find the master"! Therefore, all that a seeker can do is to be in a state of "readiness" when the master appears.

The master, who knows everything about us from his higher level of awareness and consciousness, will appear and manifest himself in such a way that the seeker will "know" that this is the time for him to be found! If a room is full of blind people who cannot see, and they are seeking a way out, they will not be able to find the door. But suddenly, the "realization" comes that one person in this group of blind people has eyes and can see! Soon, the word spreads amongst all the blind people that there is one amongst them, who can see! And then, they all run around looking for the man who has eyes! The man with eyes simply sits and watches all this! The man who has eyes can "see" what the blind men are doing. But, they think that they will somehow be able to find the one who can see .... the "seer"! And when the man with eyes sees that somebody is sincere

167

and is really making a lot of effort, going round and round the room so many times, he has compassion on that man. He steps in front of him and stretches out his hands, and the blind man catches them and says, "I have found you! I knew that one day I would find you!" This is what we all do! If the guide, if the master, is truely awakened; if he has the "eyes" to see, surely he has been watching us and has let us "find" him when we were ready! What is this state of "readiness" in which we can be found? The state of readiness is the state of "intense longing" to be one! As this longing increases, we become more and more ready. And when this longing becomes intense, we are found! This means that the master "knows" us from within. He knows what is going on in our "inner" longings, in our "inner" feelings. If he does not know, he is no master . . . . no guru. And if he knows our inner feelings, he must be there . . . . "inside" us! Therefore, the "real" master is truly "within" you! The truth is that the guide is finding us from within ourselves! That is why the true guide; the true master; one who can take us across the mind is always within us, not outside! The true guide is a part of us. He is the "reality" of our own being! He is the "totality" of ourselves, hidden within our own consciousness!

His guidance comes from within, but we don't look for him within. The true master, the true guide, the person with the connection, sits within our own self — in our consciousness — within our own head, within our body, and if we are looking outside for him, what can he do? He has to come out! We are searching for the guide "outside". Nobody searches for the guide "within"! When we look within, we simply find the mind and stop there. Therefore, we again start searching outside! If we search outside, the guide who is inside, has to come outside and hold our hand and push us back inside! He says, "Here I am, now let's start the journey from here."

In this country, in Chicago, Swami Vivekananda addressed a large religious congregation in 1893. To that congregation, he said, "I tell you, whatever you are seeing is illusion, don't take it as real! What is real is within you! From within you, the reality is being "projected" out as an illusion! It is like a projector using a film to project something on a screen. Everything outside is illusion. Don't take it as real. Don't run after it!" After saying all this, he added, "But if everything outside of you is an illusion, I must also be an illusion! My words must also be an illusion! My discourse must also be an illusion! Then how come I'm telling you, in the same breath, that everything outside of you is illusion, including myself! Why should you even listen to me? If I and my words, my message, is also an illusion, why should I ask you to listen to me?" Then he answers this question himself. He says, "It is true, I'm also an illusion of the same type as everything else! My words are also an illusion of the same type as any other illusion. My message is also an illusion, as illusory as anything else that you are experiencing. But with one difference! All "other" illusions draw you and your attention to themselves and hold you here, outside! But my illusion is 'pushing' you back into yourself! It is taking you back to reality!" When this world no longer remains real to you .... when it becomes an illusion to you, the Guru will also become an illusion, he will disappear! That is why, when the disciple "awakens" .... becomes "enlightened", there is no Guru! The Guru is part of the world of illusion and now there will be no such thing as a Guru .... or a disciple! They will have become ONE!

Therefore, there is a clash of illusions. But, although the reality is within you, and has to be discovered within, you don't look within, and hence, you must find the "symbol" of that reality in this illusion. And this "symbol" is the illusion that pushes you back to the reality within! So, although the true guide, the one who can take you beyond the mind, is within you, he "appears" — symbolically — outside, in the same form as you have! Why should he appear in the same form? Why can't he appear in a form other than that of a human being? Then it would be easy to find him; and the mind would not be so confused by so many people who claim that they have the connection! We don't know what is happening and we get confused. Why does he appear like us? There is a good reason for this.

The reason is that the methodology that a master uses to help us cross our mind involves the process of love! We will never cross the realms of the mind except through love! Every effort involves ego, except the experience of love! It is only by the process of love that the "I" can disappear and the "you" can remain! In all other effort, all sadhana and all meditation, all yogic practices, the "I" gets strengthened .. "I have done so much!" And even when the "I" says, "I am a humble person, I'm nobody," it is the "I" that is humble, the ego! There is no way of dropping the "I" except by the experience of love! In love, the "I" is forgotten. It is identified with the "you". Therefore, the master, who can take us beyond the realm of the mind, who enables us to cross the barrier of ego, uses love. And it is not possible to have love for anything; any being; any other part of this creation, except for another human being! The experience of love cannot be found on this earth except between two human beings! Therefore, God has to be loved, as a human being! When you try to love something that is superior; that is not a human being, it is not called love. It is called "worship", "admiration"; "awe", it can be called anything but love! There can be no "identification" with it and love requires your capacity to identify with someone! Therefore, the form of the guide, of the master, must look like us so that we can communicate with him, so that we can love him! He should be just like

170

us, a human being! If he is any different, we can worship him but we cannot love him! And unless we have the experience of love, we cannot "transcend" the walls created by the ego and the mind.

The master uses only one method to take us beyond the realm of the mind and that is the method of love! He has no other method. His method is to bring love into your heart, and through that, make you forget the "I" and push you back to your inner self which is the reality within you! That is his method. When he puts love in your heart, you will not even know how it happened! You are so used to the ego saying, "I want to love somebody"! If you feel that by "thinking" you can love somebody, it will never happen! "Thinking" is the antithesis of love! Yet, this is all that you know. Therefore, you ask, "How can I love the master? How can I love God? I will try very hard!" When you try hard with the mind; with your thoughts, you remain far away from love! That is why a famous Persian mystic has said, "Love is first born in the heart of the beloved". Don't make the mistake of thinking that a "lover" can love, that you can love! Something must happen at the other end which "creates" love! Take the simple man-woman relationship. If a woman is very beautiful and a man looks at her, and she doesn't look back at him, he will not experience love although he may admire her and appreciate her beauty! But if she turns around and smiles, something else starts happening. Love is spontaneous. It cannot be calculated. You have to "allow" it to happen to you .... to be given to you. But the "you", ... the "ego" is not needed! You cannot "make" love! You cannot do anything about it. And the more you try, the more you will miss! Love is not technological! The problem is not how to "do" it, the problem is to drop this effort to manufacture it; to let love "flow" into your being! Therefore, it is from the "other end" that love starts! And the same thing

171

happens in "spiritual" love with the master. It comes from him, although it looks as though we are giving the love!

When such a master comes, he enables us to find the broken pieces of the plates; the separated male and female; he makes us "transcend" the region of the mind, and gives us the experience of union! The experience of yoga, of oneness! But, even "oneness" is not the correct word to use to describe this experience! Because, when we use the word "oneness", it means that the experience of the "many" is wrong and of the "one" is right! In fact, this oneness is the "opposite" of the many! Therefore, it is still within the realm of the pairs of opposites! "One" is the opposite of "many". It does not transcend the male and female principle! The correct word to use for that state of consciousness, which is beyond the mind, is "totality". The state where everything is total! Everything is there, including the "one" and the "many"! In this state, there is no distinction between the one and the many; there is no distinction between the "creator" and the "creation", consciousness is total! The highest level of consciousness, totality, is where all levels of creation, all levels of consciousness, become one single experience! It becomes whole, complete and, therefore, is called "total". There is nothing else left! This, then, is the way in which union is achieved. The symbolic principle of the male and female experience, which is going on here, is intended to "push" us on the real union of the "separated" and the "one" becoming "total"!

172

XIX

PROBLEMS OF ETHICS

IN this chapter, I would like to share with you some ideas on the ethical questions that have always bothered mankind. If I were asked to select the most important single cause of unhappiness and misery, I would select the "guilt" complex! "I have committed sin; I have done something wrong!" In saying and feeling this way, a human being punishes himself far more effectively than any agent of God could ever do! And, we are all punishing ourselves! But is it necessary to punish ourselves to the extent that we do? Is it really necessary to have this guilt complex? Is the ethical question so overriding that we cannot get rid of it? These are some of the questions that I have often posed to myself when I consider the problems of ethics in terms of human consciousness. Is there, indeed, any "absolute" ethics at all or is it simply a social phenomenon? Are we being exploited by a set of social codes and their makers? Is society trying to control and overwhelm us by laying down these so-called "moral codes" or is there some such thing as "absolute" good and evil to which we must conform? If we do good, we are rewarded, and if we do something evil we are punished . . . What is the "reality" of the whole notion of ethics? I will attempt to give you an answer to these questions based upon the research that has been done on this subject by the Eastern philosophers who have practised the art of self-realization.

Let us first examine what makes man "moral". This is not the first time that this question is being examined. It has been examined for centuries all over the world. And, the answers that have been found, are basically the same. The basic cause which makes man a moral-conscious being is the fact that he has the "illusion" of free will! A man "thinks" then there would be no question of ethics, of right or wrong. If a man knew that God alone knows and does everything, than there would be no question of ethics, of right or wrong. The moment a man knows that he is helpless in the hands of God, there would be no question of good or evil!

But since man believes that he has the power to make choices; to choose certain alternatives open to him, it is the exercise of this illusory free will that makes him a moral man. Morality, therefore, arises directly from the experience of free will! The moment we feel we are free to choose, we become moral! We then have to choose the "right" thing to do! Once we feel that we have the "ability" to select one option in preference to the other, we become "moral" creatures! And, the question of ethics, of "right" and "wrong", begins from this point onwards. If, indeed, it is true that man has no free will, then it is also true that he can have no morality!

Therefore, these two questions, the question of whether there is any absolute ethics or not, and whether there is any absolute free will or not, are inter-related. If man had no free will, he could neither be moral nor immoral. This question of ethics has been examined by many philosophers, and the German philosopher, Kant, rightly said, "It is this illusion of free will, the illusion that we can do this or that, that makes man immoral and moral and distinguishes him from all other animals, because no other animal has the "discrimination" to choose between alternatives! All other

174

living things react to situations through instinct, intuition, or knowledge. It is only man; only one single being . . . the human being, who reacts differently! He reacts through "reason", discrimination, choice-making, "free-will" and, therefore, becomes a moral-conscious being." It is only when we exercise these special features in human consciousness that morality comes into being. The gods and goddesses, according to Indian pantheism, have no morality because they are all knowing! They know what will happen! How can there by any "good" or "evil" if you already know what is going to happen? The lower animals, below the level of man, have no morality because they can only follow their instincts! These instincts have been implanted in them by God and we never say that a dog or goat is immoral or that a cow is moral; we don't even consider the matter because how can they have any moral values when they have no choice? They are just behaving according to their instincts!

Therefore, unless you have this "special" ability to discriminate between right and wrong, between alternatives, unless you can choose, you cannot be moral! It is the human mind that makes us a chooser! It is the cause of all man's problems, both personal and social! The human mind prevents man from remaining choiceless. Life becomes a tension between opposites, between what is right and what is wrong.

It is amazing that throughout the entire creation, from the smallest particle of dust up to God Himself, there is only one moral being in this whole set-up, . . . the human being! Nobody else is bothered by morality except the human being! And not only is he moral, but he has made morality the very basis and purpose of his life! With the result that he spends his whole life in the pursuit of morality. And, the more he tries to become moral, the more unhappy he feels! The more guilty and hypocritical he feels. And, people go on cultivating and inventing false morality in order to assuage their guilt feelings! On the outside, they become great moralists. Publicly, they are able to force themselves to do only that which is right, but it is a "forced" doing! It is not spontaneous—it is not a product of their being! It is a mask behind which they are hiding! Nevertheless, they remain the same persons deep down inside. Their morality is just on the surface, something very superficial and pseudo. Inside, they are just the opposite of what they appear to be. They are hypocritical, schizophrenic! Due to this cultivated false morality, the whole of humanity has become hypocritical. It has become almost a necessity that you don't show your reality, that you go on deceiving yourself as well as everyone else. Hence, the guilt for living a false life goes on festering inside your being! And guilt, as I said, is the greatest punishment that we inflict upon ourselves! It is not even necessary for any judicial system to be set up to punish man, because every man carries within himself a "judge" which punishes him much more severely than any court . . the guilt complex!

There is no way out for a human being to escape from the experience of free will! No man can say, "Everything is destined, I can't do anything", because when one says this, one says it out of free will! He had the option to say, "I have my own mind, I can do what I like"! But, he "chose" not to say that; he "chose" to say that "everything is destined!" What makes the person say, "I believe that everything is predetermined"? How did he select this "particular" thought? How did this very process of "deciding" to prefer predetermination to free will happen? Even the rejection of free will is done "freely" out of one's free will! Those who feel that there is no free will and reject it have done it out of their own free will! Not only is "free will" a real experience, it is an inevitable one! Even if you wish to, you can't get away from the experience of free will!

Every action, every deliberation, every thought of man, is based upon free will. It has so strong a hold upon us that, even if we wish to, we cannot get away from the moral experience! Since moral experience makes us feel guilty and unhappy and since free will leads to the experience of morality, it follows that it is actually the experience of free will which makes us all unhappy! So often we say, "We are so confused, we don't know what to decide", and this is what causes unhappiness! The "right" decision is only a theoretical possibility! Only once in a while does a man really have the "feeling" of doing the right thing! Man goes through life like a tightrope-walker, continuously moving from one extreme decision to another. From this to that. From one uncertainty to another! Almost all his actions are shrouded in doubt, uncertainty, and hence great confusion! This confusion is being created by the moral dilemma, "I don't know what is right or what is wrong, what should I do? I don't know if I have been doing the right thing." When a person does not know what he is doing is right or wrong, then the guilt complex not only grips him, but also affects all those around him! By saying, "I didn't mean to hurt you; you made me do it, I didn't mean it," the guilt of the act or the thought is pushed upon others who have been quite innocent, pure and unaffected! They are also made to feel guilty, . . . sinful! We are all making ourselves miserable, punishing ourselves and others, with this feeling of guilt for having done the wrong thing! How can we know what is right? Is there a particular method by which we can always be right?

Even if we are moral beings; even if morality is inevitable; even if we cannot get away from the question of morality, away from the experience of morality, why can't we "just" be right in the first place? We ought to be able to know and do the right thing! What makes us confused? If we are so aware of morality, then we should always do the right things! So, why do we do things which are wrong? The answer is that the moral code, which defines what is right and wrong, is a code which we do not accept! The moral code has never been accepted by man! The moral code is simply a social device invented by people who want to control mankind in a particular way! Society forces us to follow it! If we do not, we cannot live, we cannot survive, we will be made to feel guilty and wrong! We must do only that which society wants us to do. Everything else must be kept locked up inside us. And, when we don't conform to it we feel guilty! We all want to show that we are following the existing moral code. But inwardly, none of us is following it! We are nonconformists to the moral code inside our hearts! The moral code is laid down by society, not by God! These codes have not been made by God! They have varied with each civilization. As the history of man has changed, the moral codes have changed. If there were a "true" moral code, it would have persisted through the ages. But it has kept on changing! Every age, every generation, it has changed and the pace of change has picked up even more in recent centuries. With this kind of change taking place in these moral codes, we can clearly see that it is simply a social phenomenon! Morality is a pseudo phenomenon. It is created in us by society. It is a subtle form of slavery! Society teaches us what is right and what is wrong. It started teaching us its code of ethics while we were still children, before we could decide on our own what was right and what was wrong! We are conditioned by society according to its ideas. All these ideas—from our parents, from the priests, teachers, politicians—all these influences are jumbled up inside our heads! And then, throughout our lives, we go on thinking that this is what must be done in order to live a "good" life! And, if we follow the moral code, we will be rewarded, and, if not, we will be punished by our own guilty conscience! Whenever we do something that our conscience says is wrong, we automatically feel guilty, we suffer; and feel a great pain inside; we become afraid, . . . full of anxiety! But our conscience is artificial, false, . . . something arbitrary. It exists only because society does not want us to be independent, non-conforming, . . . intelligent! Hence, it fixes rules of behaviour for us; do this, don't do that! Societies are making moral codes and imposing them upon us through the church, through regulations, laws, governments. But, we don't want to follow them because we are basically nonconformists! Yet, we cannot afford to ignore them, with the result that we try to become conformists although we want to be nonconformists!

Our inner life is actually nonconformist but our "appearance" is conformist; hence, the tension and the feelings of guilt! We build up this tension in us merely because of the need to "conceal" our real self! The need to "hide" ourselves from public exposure is so strong that we don't want to be ourselves, even for our own sake! We not only hide ourselves from others, but also from our own selves! We are afraid of looking at our own selves! We are afraid because we are not moral! And this hurts, because even though we can't be ourselves, even though we try to suppress our so-called immoral selves, we are basically moral! Therefore, problems come up again and again, and we remain unhappy, tense and confused!

What happens as a result of this tension? Most of our vital conscious energy, the capacity in consciousness to clearly see things and know what has to be done, is lost in the struggle going on in the sub-conscious. This struggling with nonconformity and battling with the human mind, which wants to go against the moral code, saps up all our human strength! We then become "mental" weaklings. We lose our personality and our spiritual and conscious strength

179

because of this conflict with morality—the conflict of living a life which is not really moral, and yet pretending that it is! But the consequence is far more damaging and serious than we realize on the surface. It is not confusion, but the weakening of human consciousness, the loss of our conscious strength, that is the most harmful. We become weak and are unable to cope up with the problems of life confronting us. Since we are unable to answer the moral question of right or wrong, we are unable to answer any other questions! The result is that we become stupid, tense, non-participating members of society! We become members who do not know what ought to be done! And this situation arises from the simple fact that we have a human mind and the capacity to reason.

Human reason, the use of logic, has put us in a state where, because of the experience of free will and the inevitability of morality that goes with it, we are creating a nightmare of confusion for ourselves! This situation is not hypothetical, it is a very grave and real matter! It is not a novel that we are reading, about someone else! Neither is it a philosophy! I'm talking about something which is happening to us and we all know it! You know exactly what I'm talking about because it is happening to you! Life is like a nightmare in which we are half awake and half asleep! We see a little bit, and yet everything seems to be dark; our experiences are just like shadows moving in the darkness! There is no clarity, no light . . . no certainty as to what we must do. This is the state of our existence. I would like to suggest a few measures as to what we should do in order to rescue ourselves, to overcome the dilemma that morality creates; and to give a clear guideline as to what "absolute" morality is, if there is any.

I have indicated that the use of reason, without adequate knowledge of our own past, without adequate knowledge of our genetic endowments, creates the "illusion" of free will. If we knew what genetic propensities we have inherited, from our fathers, forefathers, and ancestors, and if we could remember all the events which have taken place in our lives from birth until now, we would have enough knowledge to know exactly what to do next! There would be no ignorance, no confusion, no hesitation! It is the absence of this knowledge of our genetic propensities; and of how our environment has created certain propensities in us to act in a certain way, that makes us feel we are freely selecting one option or the other! I'll give you a small example. Suppose you place a cup of tea and a cup of coffee before a person and say, "Now what would you like to have? Tea or coffee?" The person can take tea or coffee, or neither. By saying a simple thing like "I'll have tea or coffee or neither", the man is exercising free will! But how does he select? What does "free decision", free thinking, the free will to take one or the other, mean? If he really acted freely, what would he do? He would freely choose that which he likes! Free will means freely taking that which you like, which you prefer, which your "preference" indicates!

Now, how does this preference arise? Why does someone like tea and not coffee? This is due to two sets of circumstances, two sets of factors of preference. One is based upon his genetic tendencies. His father may have liked tea, his grandfather may have liked tea, this strain is in his genes and, therefore, he likes tea! The second factor is environment. He has been brought up with tea drinkers; his cohorts like tea, his father likes tea, his brother likes it, and so on. Thus, either the genetic factors or the environmental factors govern choice-making and preferences; there is no third category! Every factor that is responsible for a person's preference for one thing or the other can be traced to either the genetic category, i.e., his hereditary propensities or to the acquired or environmental category!

181

The surprising thing is that both these factors are fixed! No change can be made in them! You can't change your birth; you can't change your ancestory and genetics. You can't change the environment which has influenced you right up to the point where the choice is being made between tea, coffee or neither! The fact is, you are choosing by factors which are fixed at that very moment of choice! If these factors of choice are fed into a computer, the computer can predict, tell in advance, that you will "freely" choose tea out of your free will! You will exercise free will and choose the tea. This may seem contradictory, but it is not really so. When we talk of "free will", we are talking of the "free exercise" of these built-in preferences! Free will is "free" only to the extent that it looks free! And why does it look free? When all the factors of choice are predetermined, why does the selection between tea and coffee seem "free"? Why do we still think, in our consciousness and awareness, that we have the capacity to "choose" between tea and coffee, when, in fact, it is predetermined by these factors of choice in advance? The reason why we still feel that we have exercised our free will is because we are ignorant of these factors of choice. At the moment of making the choice, we are not free! We can just press a button and the computer will tell us, "According to your preferences, you are bound to "freely" choose coffee". Our behaviour is like a chain in which every step is determined by the past. Our future is not really the "future"! It is just a by-product of the past. It is only the past influence of these factors of choice which is determining, shaping, formulating and conditioning our actions.

B. F. Skinner says that man is as predictable as anything else. The only problem is that we have not yet devised the means and methods to know his "total" past! The moment we can know what these past factors of choice are,

182

we can predict every action of a person! Everything that has ever happened to us is connected with our actions; so obviously, free will is simply an illusion. But, on the other hand, if somebody else selects the tea or coffee for me, then it is not free will for me because somebody else's will is being imposed! What I will freely do can be predicted in advance, but what another person will suggest to me is unpredictable! The fact of the matter is that, it is the use of the human mind in selecting between options that creates the "illusion" of free will. This illusion is sustained by our "ignorance" of the factors of choice; with the result, that the "experience" of free will seems real! Free will as such may not be real but the "experience" of free will is real! We really "feel" that we can freely take tea or coffee because we don't know how or why we select it. It is this ignorance, plus the use of reason, which gives us this capacity of free will. It is only by "thinking" that we can deliberate upon the choices open to us! It is necessary to think about them, and then only, do we come to a "decision" to do this or that. And the more we think, the more free will we use!

When we really want to make up our minds, to "decide" things for ourselves, we think very hard! And, when we keep on thinking over and over, "shall I do this or that? To do or not to do? To be or not to be?", the more "freely" are we "willing" what we will do! It is the thinking process, plus the ignorance of the factors or preference, that leads to the experience of the illusion of free will! It also leads to the inevitable experience of morality! When we act without using reason, we are not "haunted" by feelings of guilt, of having done something wrong. If something happens to us, accidentally, we can excuse ourselves. We didn't do it! We didn't "think" about it, it never came from us, it just happened! We are excused and our conscience doesn't punish us! It is only when we have thought and thought and thought and then done something which went wrong, that we punish ourselves! It becomes our responsibility then, our decision! If we didn't "decide" to do it, we wouldn't feel guilty!

People often ask me, "Can there be a combination of destiny and free will?" And the answer given by the Eastern philosophers and practitioners of self-realization is, yes! In life, there are some events which happen accidentally, without predetermination, without pre-deliberation, without thinking, and to which no guilt is attached! When something happens, say, without your will, without your thinking, no morality is attached to it! But when you "think" and do a thing, morality gets connected to it! The distinction between destiny and free will is based on this device. When you do not even have the choice of thinking about a matter, you cannot be responsible! If you did not "decide" what to do, how can you be responsible? How can you be rewarded or punished for something that "you" haven't done? On the other hand, when you clearly see the options or the alternatives open to you, and "choose" one in preference to the other, you are fully responsible and are, therefore, rewarded or punished! Morality, then, is linked only with that part of human experience where reason is used, and nowhere else! It is only when we use reason, only when we use our mind, that the question of morality comes up. If we use something other than the mind, there would be no question of morality; there would be no question of guilt. But is there anything else that we use? If there is something in consciousness that we can use, we can get out of the moral dilemma. The practitioners of the art of self-discovery have discovered that there is, indeed, a reliable, permanent and conscious part of ourselves which can be used to overcome this problem of morality. I have already mentioned in the previous chapters that this part in our consciousness, above the mind, is described as the soul of man, it is the real core of human consciousness! It is that part of human consciousness over which the mind functions as a cover. The mind frames our conscious experiences into time, space, and causation. When we have an experience in the frame of time, space, and causation, it is an experience being had through mind and reason. And if we can have an experience outside this frame, it would still be our personal and conscious experience, but it would not be an experience of reason!

When reason is not used, the illusion of free will does not occur. Therefore, the moral question does not arise! And since we are capable of using that part of consciousness which does not rely upon the mind, we are indeed capable of attaining a state of consciousness that is not tied down by morality! The whole moral dilemma arises only because of the use of the mind and reason! "Should I do this or should I do that"? This question of choosing between alternatives does not occur in the experience of the soul . . . of higher consciousness. Whenever a certain need or situation occurs, our soul, this higher state of consciousness, will automatically respond! Our actions become spontaneous, intuitive and no thinking is required! Consciousness in itself is enough! There is no need to follow any moral code! This so-called moral code is very arbitrary, very artificial! It gives us a fixed pattern to follow, a fixed "gestalt". But life goes on flowing and changing! Life is very uncertain, and does not follow any logical pattern. It is basically "supra-logical", without reason, . . . irrational! And unless all "thinking" and deciding with the mind, with the intellect, is dropped, unless we become more conscious, more alert, . . . we will simply remain slaves to some moral code! We will always require a moral code to guide us through life!

With the development of human awareness, not only are we freed from the painful and unnecessary experience of guilt, but we are also able to resolve the MORAL DILEMMA, and life takes on an expanded meaning and new significance—permitting us to to live it to its fullest! We eventually arrive at the totality of everything . . . within and without! We regain the source of all knowledge . . . and more! We achieve a higher state of consciousness wherein all mysteries are unfolded and duality is transformed into oneness!

XX

TOTAL MORALITY

MORAL principles are absolute and their relativity comes in contrast with their absoluteness. Morality is an active attitude towards social relationship born of any accepted point of view in life either by an individual or society, or by both.

Morality in society is an expression of its superegoistic presuppositions. That 'Cow is sacred and has to be respected' is a moral commandment, and irrespective of whether one knows the reason thereof — normally one does not even try to know it — he obeys it because that has been the unquestioned outlook of the society one has been brought up in. An individual acts 'morally' not because he could justify it rationally but because that has been a constituent of the social attitudes to which he meekly, and often unknowingly, submits. Morality does not seem to be for him an outcome of any deliberate attempt to refine his socio-individual personality but an inevitable consequence of superegoistic presuppositions in the formation of which he has little or no part to play.

Some refuse or do not want to follow or find faults with the beaten track and try to evolve a moral code which they claim to be a formulation of their supra-rational revelations. Such few endeavour to change or alter the prevalent social morality and substitute the same by a different order. Thus, Prophet Mohammad influenced the then society and introduced different notions in place of the Vedic ritualism. Both of them claimed supra-rational revelations as the source of their different outlooks which sought to replace or at least to change the older order.

Morality is sought to be justified on the ground of its being conducive to personal and social weal. If attachment to alcohol is deemed to be immoral it is on account of its being injurious to personal and consequent social health. Similarly, respect for cow is explained in terms of her utility to society, which in the course of generations comes to be accepted as an unquestioned moral attitude though the followers may not know the justification thereof. Those who tend to defy all accepted norms of moral behaviour have no hesitation in accepting — rather they do accept — the patterns of behaviour of individuals in the interest of social welfare. The social reformers in various ages seem to have tried to rebuild moral structures of the respective societies upon rational justification, though their reformation may be deemed to be unjustifiable.

Morality is not an independent source. It is a cluster of social impressions to which an individual is unconsciously and yet persistently exposed by virtue of his being a constituent of the particular social order. The personality of an individual is normally an outcome of such impressions and very few might escape them successfully. An individual in a society is 'habitually' moral and indeliberately 'right' or 'wrong'. His morality springs from blind adherence to the accepted moral standards of society. A vast majority follows the beaten track. A moral act done without any clear evaluation of it by the agent becomes an act of 'trust' or faith or habit but does not appear to be a moral act if such an act does not involve an active and meaningful participation of the free agent therein.

Scientific, unrealised and unrealisable truths are blindly accepted by a commoner. Blind acceptance of a moral code by him need not and should not remain open to singular criticism. But the difference between the two is clear. The scientific proposition, i.e., 'milk contains protein', is information, the blind acceptance of which and action thereon does not affect the moral personality. Besides, such a proposition is always open to and based upon rational justification. In the case of blind acceptance of moral structure the very freedom of choice, which is deemed to be of paramount basic value in such an act, is mortgaged, and thereby the 'morality' of an act tends to evaporate.

Morality is always relative to the point of view it is based upon. The possibility or even presence of disagreement amongst the members of the same society or of different societies in respect of any moral code is apparent enough to be overlooked lightly. It tends to point out that morality is relative in nature and absolute morality, if any, is unrealisable.

A moral principle which is absolute, irrespective of age, society and point of view, is yet to be known. The patterns of moral behaviour, the principles underlying are seen to vary in the same society at different times. Thus, for example, dating is a normal, morally approved, system in Western countries while the same is looked upon with moral disapproval elsewhere. The codes of morality change, giving place to new ones which may at times be totally different from, or even contradictory to, those previously held. Morality always appears to be relative.

The principle of morality remains absolute, though its expressions in different societies and ages could and do differ.

Expressions remain relative, the principle underlying them is absolute. Changes in dresses do not invalidate the principle that the body should be protected from the forces of nature by wearing clothes. Such a view appreciably tries to clarify that absoluteness and relativity of morality are not really contradictory and that they could thus be synthesized.

The principle of regulating sex relation is not an absolute principle, and least the moral principle. Such a regulation is born of certain social necessities which themselves are an outcome of a certain point of view in respect of social weal adopted by any society. The absolute principle is not absolute, it is relative to the adopted point of view of a respective society at a given period.

It is governed by the concept of social good. This 'good' is also not absolute in the sense that its contents have changed and continue to change with the march of circumstances. The 'good' is neither absolute nor does it appear to possess any intrinsic value.

The 'good' may not be morally approved by a person brought up under a different social order. To claim any intrinsic worth for 'good' would also appear to be more an outcome of some undefined and indefinable personal convictions than a result of justifiable ratiocination.

Then there is the aspect of morality and mental health. Functional morality, in contradistinction to ideal morality, considerably depends upon the mental health of individuals. The intellectual knowledge of morality does not lead to commensurate moral actions. Unless a piece of knowledge becomes an integral part of the total reflective-behavioral apparatus of the individual, it is not able to bridge the gap between knowledge and profession on the one hand and practice on the other. If the gap between knowledge and practice remains, it makes for a damaging situation of deceit and hypocrisy, lowering individual and public standards of conduct.

Basically, morality means high quality of human relations, i.e., treating others as persons and not as things within the framework of equality, justice, non-violence and larger and deeper sympathies. The chance of both reflective and conventional morality flourishing is high if the mental health of the people is sound. With poor mental health, on the other hand, the chances of poor moral perception go up, prescriptive morality runs the danger of being miscarried, moral prescription lends itself to acceptance of irrational principles, and moral command conditions habits of obedience out of timidity or insecurity. It is not intended to maintain that morality depends on any single factor. Moral action is a consequence of a number of factors conflicting among themselves. In the modern 'sick' society the ethical implications of mental health require improving the moral health of the people.

Mental health is a complexity rooted in the physical, the social and the personal being of man. In any case, it is an index of the quality of living, causing one to attach specific meanings to objects and persons and to inter-personal relations of conflict, co-operation and indifference. A mentally healthy person develops a certain minimum degree of self-thinking, self-discipline and self-direction. He has a certain minimum level of detachment and objectivity to be able to enjoy both the states of his own mind and his relations with the outside world. He succeeds in striking comparatively an integration within himself and without.

Any culture that skilfully endeavours to keep conflict and frustration in trim so that the mill of unethical power keeps grinding relentlessly gives a lie to intrinsic moral values. For, even political power, such as it be as a value, has no claim to ethical status unless it functions under the tutelage of morality. Poor mental health, inter alia, breeding as it does conflict, frustration and the rest, is at once a moral loss. A clear-cut line has to be drawn between the pathological conflict and a moral health conflict. Such a noble conflict as arises out of human urge to forge moral progress is of a different genre from the pathological conflict that feeds on personal insecurity, hatred and social injustice. The former has a constructive role in morality while the latter a destructive one. The potentialities of sound mental health are not reckoned with, particularly by the revolutionaries swearing by violence. Because mental health and violence would prove to be contradictory, social and moral ill, from the gross crime to subtle jealousy, hatred and mad pursuit of power can be easily blamed on poor mental health. A confident and self-secure person would not fly to rage or crime, nor would have a neurotic urge for unreasonable jealousy, hatred and authoritarian power. The sharp teeth of power have an insatiable lust for all the sweet things of life which alone make life meaningful and worth living. But, to be sure, authoritarianism as a compulsive style of life of an individual or of politics matches more the inner hollowness than the legitimate demands of one's station or office.

Mental health has reference to persons whose enhanced powers of mind enable them to face the modern challenges of knowledge and life, helping them to give the right direction to personal and social life in behalf of rationally sound moral values.

What robs mental health and morality both is selfishness, incapacitating the individuals to see human relations in the proper perspective and thereby denying them the satisfying emotions attendant on sharing and co-operation. Often rugged individualism is justified in the name of freedom which has long been in the making in human history, both as a value and practice.

Freedom is a necessary condition of mental health and morality. For, without it self-discipline, self-direction and self-choice have a remote chance of realization. Without it neither the correct self-image nor a correct image of others is possible, and both are otherwise essential for the moral quality involved in inter-personal relations and attitudes to reciprocity of the individuals. Freedom as such, as a principle and force of transcendence, has its roots in the maturity of individuals and has to be achieved creatively. Accordingly, freedom and rugged individualism or selfishness are contradictory. Practice of freedom is rare due both to cultural and personal short-comings. What passes for freedom generally is licentious conduct individually or even on a mass scale, at times, under the garb of philosophically sanctified ideologies. The charge on a culture and the individual, first of all, is to ensure the best conditions of freedom which in turn become the means to ever greater freedom of an individual in behalf of self-growth and social progress. Unless both self-development and social progress are rationally integrated, freedom in our sense of the term becomes meaningless. And, this cannot be done all too easily for reasons of deep-seated conventional habits of thought and living, including inevitably vested interests of all sorts. A vigorous and rational individual and social action towards desirable social change do emerge as the inevitables of the logic of the situation.

Social reconstruction, in the nature of things, cannot be done with one stroke. It calls for a deep understanding of interlocking personal and social forces, an experimental and rational approach of all sentimentality and unexamined pre-

193

suppositions. Progress in knowledge and historical forces have forced an urgency for the vigorous reconstruction of culture before it is too late. While the economic factor claims priority, so that, first of all, the economic basis of society is justly ordered and reasonable equality of income ensured to all individuals, it would be a utopian claim to maintain that the rest of the ills of an individual and society would evaporate at the magic touch of economic equality. Human ego is much too complicated and vainglorious to rest content with economic equality. In view of the available knowledge of human psychology it is impossible to establish a one-to-one correlation between economic equality and sound mental health. All the non-economic elements, therefore, have to be pressed into service through acculturisation and broad-based education, formal and informal, to disabuse man of greed, lust and power. Even economic growth cannot be successfully achieved through purely economic means. It has to galvanise the social purpose of the individuals and to win them into an enterprise of co-operation and high motivation for production before people can enjoy its fruits.

If poverty is detrimental to mental health, no less is affluence and its erratic distribution over a small section of society. Both poverty and affluence have been accepted, with the result that a rational approach to the production and distribution of wealth and all it implies in terms of recording of status hierarchy and human relations, is at best a poor show. Similarly, technology has come to acquire, wittingly or unwittingly, the status of an end. And, the lightning speed with which it has blasted the age-old habits and customs has thrown the moral world out of gear, enveloping it with a thick fall-out of confusion. This wilful technology is identified as one major cause of the cancer of mind. The oppressive technology is causing an almost neurotic reaction to it, sending many people reeling nostalgically to the dream-land of pre-technological civilization.

It is highly doubtful if one of the basic problems of humanity can be eradicated without both high and medium technology as the specific need be. Now, without it, is it possible to maximise leisure, which is indispensable for freedom, and personal growth, granting of course that people be properly educated for availing of leisure creatively? It does need, however, all the powers of the mind and the best of planning to subdue technology to desirable human ends so that all kinds of goods, including economic and political power, have a chance of fair distribution making for a healthy, dialogic, face-to-face community, away from the monolithic society of faceless individuals.

The world has never been without violence, there has never been a worship of violence on such a large scale as today. What was considered a sort of helplessness in human nature is being gradually turned into a positive value; all kinds of pseudophilosophies are being pressed into service to justify violence as an arch-value for social change. Therein lurks the catastrophe and, equally, the challenge for mankind. For, peace may no longer be viewed as an ultimate goal but an immediate necessity without which civilization may not survive.

An understanding of the implications of sound mental health in the service of morality suggests a limited focus on the enormous problems of violence and peace. Mere echoing of values, however noble, may not go very far. Nor may any insight into the problem of peace, however meaningful, cut much ice unless the mind is healthy enough to profit by values and insights.

Mental health itself is partly nurtured by lofty values. The historical and psychological experience demands that an attack be made to ensure mental health to the people in this ever growing "acquisitive society" smarting under runaway technology. It is imperative that a continuous appraisal of our culture be made in terms of physical, interpersonal and socio-political environment, right from the family through school to the world at large.

A full-fledged programme of mental health, with a sound philosophy to back it, needs to be integrated with formal and informal education of the people. Such a programme must aim at educating the emotions and reason of the people and cultivate the things of the mind without which freedom and sanity would always be in danger. Much of the violence of the modern world seems to be due to ontological devitalization of our society. Mental health must succeed in restoring spiritual vitality to make this world safe for peace and efflorescence.

XXI

MORAL OBLIGATION

THE concept of moral obligation arises from a relationship between two persons. A reference to something for which one is obliged to the other may not be stated in our linguistic contexts, but this can always be made explicit if required. The proposition that the concept of moral obligation is interpersonal excludes the possibility of its being used in situations in which solitary persons are involved. It makes no sense to say that Robinson Crusoe, morally speaking, has any obligations to discharge.

Common usage allows expressions like "moral obligation", "legal obligation", "social obligation". When we use these expressions, we know what we are talking about. We know, also, that by doing so we continue to maintain and promote clarity in our interpersonal communication. This fact of life is enough to show that not all obligation is moral and that there are other sorts of obligation as well. The relation between moral and social obligation is: as morality operates within society, all moral obligation must, at the same time, be social obligation. Thus, social obligation is perfectly compatible with moral obligation. Since both moral and non-moral obligations exhaust the entire universe of social obligation, non-moral obligation, too, is compatible with social obligation. Whenever moral obligation obtains, social obligation must also obtain; but it is never the case that every case of social obligation entails moral obligation.

The relation between obligation and ought is that of necessary implication. But the converse of this relation is not true. The reason for this is that the concept of obligation is narrower than the concept of ought. It belongs to what has been called the secondary field of morality, not to the primary field of morality as the concept of ought does. Obligation arises when the moral balance between two persons is upset by the actions of one of them. The obligation is discharged when the moral equilibrium is restored by the actions of the one who disturbed it. When we say we are under an obligation to someone we mean that we ought to restore the moral equilibrium by "discharging our obligation". To discharge one's obligation is to restore the moral equilibrium. Doing so terminates the special moral relationship created between the two people by the upset of the moral balance which gave rise to the obligation. The concept of obligation entails the concept of ought. The relation between the two concepts is of the same order as that which obtains between the sentences: "This is red" and "This is coloured". The first sentence entails the second.

Obligation operates within the context of rules and directives so that, if there are no rules, there can be no obligation. Moral rules are those rules which prohibit certain types of behaviour. For instance, 'Aid those in distress', and 'Thou shalt not kill' are primary rules of morality. Moral rules are those rules which prohibit certain types of behaviour in response to some upset of the moral balance. For example, 'An eye for an eye' is a secondary rule of morality. An obligation is created whenever any primary rule of morality is violated. Three conditions for obligation arise: (i) There must be rules or standards of behaviour. (ii) These rules or standards are treated as supporting demands. (iii) It is also necessary that these rules must have been violated, resulting in an upset of moral balance, so that the discharge of obligation could restore the moral balance.

A moral rule is so called because it is required or adopted from the moral point of view. The moral point of view is not solely the agent's point of view. It is doing things on principle, and materially it is doing them for the good of everyone alike. The moral point of view regards a moral rule as overriding not only inclination but also self-interest.

XXII

MORALS FOR MYSTICAL LIFE

MORALITY is concerned with the determination of the highest good of man and with the appropriation of that ideal. The way to this ideal is the moral path or the path of virtue. Those who are satisfied with a description of this ethical life are moral scientists. Those who cannot rest satisfied with a mere description of normal life but insist on an explanation of it are moral philosophers. The latter require the derivation of the moral law from metaphysical foundations. Those who do not want to separate the region of nature from the region of grace cannot stop at the derivation of the moral law; they maintain that morality culminates in mysticism or direct vision of God. This moral life is only part of the richer life which receives its sap from a metaphysical root and yields a mystical fruit.

We define moral ideal as the realisation of the highest reality, namely, God, and consequently define virtue as that which leads to such a realisation. This solves many problems of morality. Life presents many situations where the practice of even cardinal virtue like truth or non-violence leads to conflicts. If one practises truth one may have to forgo non-violence and one has to take resort to casuistry. But if virtue is defined not as a value in itself but as an instrument of God realisation, this difficulty disappears. He alone who has received illumination can find a way out of a casuistical situation.

Real illumination cannot be achieved without performing duties. Renunciation which stresses knowledge cannot be reached without Karma or action. The path of knowledge and the path of disinterested action are not independent. Knowledge is not mere information but transformation of behaviour.

The virtue of knowledge lies not in the discursive or logical knowledge but spiritual illumination. Morality becomes a propaedeutic to the realization of the mystical ideal, namely, the vision of God. There is no divorce between the realm of nature and the realm of ends. Now, imbibing of virtues is not an event but a process, and so morality and mysticism become almost the earlier and later stages in the one continuous process of perfection. It becomes difficult to demarcate the line where morality ends and mysticism begins. The line dividing them is a mathematical line devoid of breadth. Mysticism, which implies immediate experience of the ultimate reality, is itself a never-ending process. As long as man remains a finite creature he is limited and cannot claim complete realisation. It may take a number of lives to attain liberation. The liberation of one individual is really not complete till the liberation of all; and obviously this process would go on for ever.

Morality and mysticism are one continuous process, and if mysticism is a never-ending process then morality also is. Moral perfection is a never-ending process, because a human being as a human being can never eliminate the surd of sensibility from his life. To be completely under the control of active emotions is a never-ending process. The imbibing of virtues must be gradual because one cannot try to attain

201

to a goal which is too high; one has to go bit by bit. If you are going to achieve the ideal and if you reach perfection it means you as such are dissolved because the moment of attaining perfection is the moment of losing finitude. The very statement that you have attained to perfection is meaningless, for, where you are, perfection is not; and where perfection is, you are not. There is an antinomy in the very conception of moral life because its procedure is self-destructive. If moral life is striving against evil, one must always try to destroy evil and attain to good; at the same time, one must always try to preserve evil in order to save morality. With evil the moral task remains incomplete; without evil the moral life itself comes to an end. This is an inherent and incurable ailment of moral life and morality seems to consist in a precarious balancing exercise between the destruction and preservation of evil.

Morality is an end in itself, and to save morality from destruction means keeping alive the conflict between good and evil. It is a hopeless narrowness of view to conceive the moral ideal as merely righting of wrongs. What harm is there if the task of morality is eliminated of sensibility (as against understanding) or egoism, and is finally accomplished? The work of perfection of others still remains. It becomes the nature of a perfected saint to work disinterestedly for universal welfare. Seeing God in all beings and loving them is the essence of mysticism. Mysticism must be understood not merely as a secluded life but a life of intense love for all beings. It may be an end of morality as morality, but it is not at all undesirable. A child when he grows up into a youth, no longer remains a child: but no one on that account wishes the child not to grow and not attain to manhood. To say that morality should always remain fighting against evil is to say that we do not want morality to mature into super morality.

Religion does not displace virtues. It puts them to the service of God, and in this sense religion is super-moral. Let us not understand super-morality as something unconnected with morality, something which cannot be and need not be moral. Super-morality means morality first and foremost plus something more. It is through morality that we reach the super-moral. If the process of acquiring virtues is morality, automatic outflow of them is super-morality. Virtues become natural to him. He will not strive for virtues; but every one of his acts will reveal them. Such a perfected saint who may be said to have attained a super-moral stage becomes the standard of morality.

We cannot say that morality ends where mysticism begins. Nor can we say that morality is the cause and mysticism the effect. If there is causality between them, it is reciprocal causality. The more we advance on the path of virtue, the more will we get the vision of reality; and the more we get the vision of reality, the more is the progress in morality. They are causes of each other. Morality leads to mysticism and mysticism in its turn illumines morality. In morality virtues are acquired; in religion virtues are infused by God. The divine infusion of virtues adds a new meaning to morality. Morality is duty towards man as man; religion is duty towards man as God.

XXIII

THE MEANING OF BEING

PHILOSOPHERS have for long discussed the problems concerning the nature and knowledge of existence.

For example, the nature of particular things, such as a jar or a cap; the nature of an all prevading, modifying substance which transforms itself into all kinds of existent things; the one non-dual substratum, illusorily manifesting itself into all forms of apparently existing things, and

an attribute of things which must be,

an attribute opposed to non-existence,

an attribute of being the content of affirmative cognition,

an attribute of being the content of valid cognition or the capability of valid cognition or its relation,

the attribute of efficiency,

the state of being present, and

the attribute of universal generality.

They have discussed such questions as whether existence can be graded as noumenal, phenomenal or illusory and whether such a category as non-existent is possible. We arrive at a knowledge of existence through perception, inference or authority. Whether existence is identical with consciousness or not, it does not explain the meaning of being.

Existence as a concept is our creation. It is not a simple idea as some might think. Complex as it is, it is used in one or more of the following senses:—

(1) *Life and growth*: When we say that once there was a king, we mean that once there lived a king. The expression 'there is an oak in that garden' means that an oak is growing there.

(2) *A Certain Posture*: When we say that there is a walking stick on the table, we mean that the stick lies on the table; and when we say that there is a stick in the corner, we mean that it stands there.

(3) *Tangibility*: When we say that the tea is hot, we mean that we feel it so on touch, unless we otherwise infer that it is so. When a man in the street says that the persons he sees on the cinema screen do not exist, he simply means that he cannot touch them.

(4) *Capacity to affect* (that is, to please or cause pain): When we say that there is pain in the patient's toe, we mean that he feels it is in his toe. When a person says that there is love for his child in his heart, he means that he feels the emotion.

(5) *Characteristic motion, static condition or simply standing still*: When we say it is a railway train, we generally mean that we see it running or standing as the case may be.

(6) *The mere consciousness of a concept*: When we say 'the bear is' or 'an ant is', we simply mean that we have formed the concept of a bear or an ant.

(7) *Position and place*: My chair is here; your horse is there; there is water in the well. By these utterances one speaks of the position or place of the chair, the horse and water.

(8) *A mere coupler*: It is a link between two logical terms; that is, the subject and the predicate of a proposition, it looks like a coupler between two wagons of a railway train. The 'is' amounts, as it were, to a plus and the 'is not' to a minus. Your cap is red=your cap+redness. your cap is not red=your cap — redness.

(9) *Self-consciousness*: It is when I say I am, I become, or mean to be, conscious of my own self.

(10) *Present, past or future*: In statements the 'is', 'was' and 'will be' denote the present, past and future time, respectively.

(11) *Imposition or superimposition of (or emphasis on) an attribute felt to be inherent or otherwise*: Heaven is blissful. The Absolute is ultimate. 'This knife is good'. I call it so, although a knife is amoral. It is good if it serves my purpose, and bad if it hurts a child. So fire is a good servant but a bad master. It is serviceable when it helps cooking and evil when it burns a cottage. Thus, we impose attributes upon objects.

(12) *Identity of an object with reference to space*: This is the tree I saw three years ago. This is the river I saw last year. When I make these statements, I perceive the tree or the river as the same object, because it grows or flows at a place which has not perceptibly changed.

(13) *Identity of an object with regard to some preconceived but implicit attributes (characteristic, qualities or values)*: When I say 'This is the boy I saw fifteen years ago', I recognize the boy in spite of the many changes in him during such a long time, owing to some such characteristics in him as special

206

features, marks or qualities which I remember and still find in him.

(14) *An immediately successive and implicit repetition of experience (percept, image or concept) of an object which we believe to be one and the same*: The tree is equal to tree-tree-tree .... to an X number. Existence may, therefore, be the continued series of implicit repetition of an immediate experience or reproduction of an object. Here 'is' stands for the abbreviated form of repetition for convenience and other purposes.

(15) *A tendency originating in tradition and habit of thought*: When we refer to the ideal content of a judgement to an object beyond such a content, this outward reference may be to an object, mental or extra-mental. When there is no correspondence between the ideal content and such an object, we speak of hallucination, and when the correspondence between the ideal content and the malobserved or misobserved object is defective, we have an illusion. Both illusion and hallucination come under appearance which includes dreams also. When the correspondence is valid in what we call normal waking life we call it phenomenon. But when the correspondence is supposed to refer to some transcendental object or objects, we call it noumenon. Some thinkers like to distinguish existence from subsistence, which means to them different-order-of existence. So, to them, if a substance exists its attribute subsists.

(16) *Manifestation of an object to mind*: Existence literally means stepping out, standing out, stepping forth or standing forth. A tree may be supposed to stand still, unperceived by me, but it stands out or

steps forth to me in perception. A mystery may lie hidden from me, but it steps out when it is revealed to me. Such a manifestation may occur through perception, imagination or be revealed through intuition or under inspiration.

(17) *Recognition of an object*: It is a tree. It is hot today. In these statements, I recognize the 'it' as a tree or as hot. It is tree may mean that 'a tree is a tree'. Or the 'it' may be a logical subject. When we say that it is hot today, the logical subject may be today's temperature, however vague. Or else, the it may be the metaphysical subject which may be characterized as a concrete individual or the Ultimate Reality. Some philosophers think that the 'it' stands for that, a vague whole, or what may be characterized as perception, whereas the predicate may be characterized as what, a comparatively clear whole (determinate perception).

To identify existence with a form of perception or a category of understanding is difficult, for, it is not simple in character. It is quite complex so as to involve more or less the ideas of breathing, living, residing, standing still, time, space, identity, persistence (continuance or repetition), apprehension, manifestation or recognition, or else a combination of two or more of these ideas in different contexts.

Children and ordinary people do not seem to have the concept of existence. Babies simply use that or it when they point to the moon; or they simply say 'mother, milk' when they are hungry. They seldom use or think of 'is'. What exactly does my friend mean when he calls me (by my name simply)? Does he think of me or my existence? I know, answers can differ, but I would prefer the first alternative. When a grown-up child says that 'the coat is (is not) in the box', he means to affirm ('or deny) the association of the coat with the box as the container and the contained. Does he ever dwell on the existence of the coat or of the box, or of the relation of the coat and the box? He simply means that he either sees or does not see the coat and the 'inside of the box' together. By an object ceasing to exist, the young child means that he no longer perceives the association of the subject and the predicate, once cherished in a particular way.

Just as colour is a concept to connote the three primary or the seven prismatic colours or of their various shades and combinations, so is existence a general name and notion of the various action verbs. Think of pure existence, and you will at once think of extension or space; you will imagine or look at the expanse of the sky; you will cast a glance at your extensive lawn; you will think of life and death or of growth and destruction; or else you will concentrate on the identity of the subject and the predicate of a judgment.

Some people tend to believe that we perceive, imagine or conceive only in terms of existenc and non-existence. Just as, they say, we cannot divest a perception of its spatial form, we cannot divest an object of its existential import either.

We are so obsessed by tradition, custom, and habit of thought and language that we cannot easily get rid of the idea of existence, which we, therefore, regard as a category. The concepts of substance and attribute, too, are so engrossing that we cannot shake them off easily. Most of us conceive of a thing as a substance having attributes. We can divest an object of its attributes (at least mentally) to lay bare its hypostatis. The analogy is comfortable. But think of a solid cube of sugar, and try to strip off its sugar. What will you expose? This, too, is an analogy, though less comfortable to a believer in substance. The element of tradition, custom, habit and language also influences us in shaping our thoughts, even philosophical thoughts. While Arabic, I am told, has no present tense and no equivalent for 'is', Hindi abounds in it, rather with a vengeance.

Existence is our creation. It lives in us rather than we in it. It seems, therefore, that if one should ever think of the Ultimate Reality, one could not legitimately declare it as existent or non-existent. If it should be indicaed as something beyond the mind, could existence or non-existence be predicated of it? Could we legitimately characterise the Absolute as existent, conscious and blissful? For, it is either, both or beyond both. Whose existence or non-existence do I mean? Of my pen? Or, the concrete individual? Existence is the meeting point, as it were, of the indeterminate and the determinate elements of our experience, perception or imagination. When I perceive a chair I never perceive its existence. Existence may, therefore, be that element in perception or imagination which is inferred rather than perceived.

XXIV

'CAUSATION' : THE BUDDHIST POINT

THE Buddhists have a unique stand regarding causation. According to them, the effect is neither a manifestation of cause nor a new creation but it only replaces the cause. The effect arises in functional dependence upon a totality of causes and conditions which are its immediate antecedents. A co-existence of cause and effect is impossible. Dependence of effect upon its cause means that it replaces the previous entity, i.e., the cause. The cause is the thing—itself or the reality. The Buddhist belief is that all things are caused. The Buddhist conceptions of impermanence, universal change, non-substantiality and the theory of Karma and rebirth are all different aspects of the Buddhist Theory of Causation.

One system assumes that cause and the effect are only two stages of one thing, which only implies that there is no real causation in the sense of one entity causing another. There is no relation of logical necessity between cause and effect. The cause being there, the effect may arise, or it may not.

The second system defines cause as that which invariably precedes the effect. The cause-and-effect relation is defined in terms of temporary succession and not in terms of an extra factor in causation as distinct from the ontological status of cause. There are two factors in producing an effect: (i) the ontological nature of the thing called cause, and (ii) the time which contains that thing.

The relationship between cause and time is not essential. A thing may or may not exist in time. Moreover, even an eternal thing can be conceived without any reference to time. The relationship between the ontological status of a thing and time is only incidental. It is a contigent and not a necessary relation.

On the one hand, there is the ontologically real thing. On the other, there is time. The effect is produced by the combination of both. Thus, there are two factors in effect also: (i) the ontological status of effect and (ii) the time in which effect exists.

One system implies that effect is a new creation and it did not exist before its production. Therefore, the ontological status of effect has no relation with the ontological status of cause. As the effect did not exist before its production, it is ontologically independent of its cause. In the ontological status there is no relation, but there is relation between the time of cause and the time of effect. For the first system time is one and its division is artificial. The basis for the relation between cause and effect is time, or the relation is momentary in nature. The only type of momentary relation that could be there between cause and effect is that of succession.

Succession is of two types: (i) where the succession is from the point of view of the preceding moment, and (ii) where the succession is from the point of view of the succeeding moment. In the first case, when it is said in science that there is a cause, therefore there will be an effect, it only refers to a possible occurrence of an effect, because at the causal level effect is not ontologically involved. From the point of view of the preceding moment, there is only a possibility of the succeeding moment. Even temporarily, there is only a possibility and no necessity. In the second case, since there is effect there must have been a cause also. When something occurs, the notion of prior time also comes. But, nothing can be said about the ontologically non-existent effect in that prior time. Even at the level of effect, it is bound with its cause only through time. Time is the only factor that binds a cause and an effect. There is nothing common between the cause and the effect, except the factor of time. The relation between the cause and time was contingent. Similarly, at the level of effect the relation between effect and time is also contingent.

A limit will have to be put to our going back in time, when it is said, "Thus far, no further." But, this limit will always be arbitrary, as any limitation of time. The ontological status of cause has no bearing on the ontological status of effect. The relation between cause and effect being contingent, the notion is used only to minimise the scope of the relation. Anything prior in time to the effect could be causally related to it, had the causal relation between the cause and the effect been necessary.

In the first place, cause does not change itself into an effect. Moreover, in itself cause has no force to produce an effect. Cause stands in need of an external agent to move it. The creative force of cause is accidental. It may produce an effect, or it may not, depending upon an agent. The agent may be man or God. Because a conscious being has a free will, he may act or he may not. The creative force does not produce the necessary effect. That is why it is contingent.

There are some external realities. One reality is not responsible for the existence of the other reality, e.g., the soul is not responsible for the existence of matter. Each reality exists in its own right. That is why any kind of relationship between two eternal realities will be incidental. One atom does not depend on the other atom. It is only incidentally that two realities come in contact. Therefore, the cause-and-effect relation, and for that matter any kind of relation involving the co-presence of two things, is always contingent in the sense that the two things may not be inter-dependent, and their alleged co-presence may be due to certain external factors, like the will of God, which, being free, is again accidental.

The Creator does not evolve but only gives rise to appearance which, though entirely depending on it, does not affect it. The Creator is the cause and world the effect. The relation between the Creator and the world is inexplicable. This relationship cannot be placed under any one of the logically recognised categories. The origin of the world cannot also be explained. Whatever change takes place, it is in Maya, and is superficial. The Creator which is the cause, remains unaffected by it. This leads to the idea that causal relation is contingent.

Causality exists between two moments, it rests on infer-ence. The concept of one involves that of the other, and ultimately both the concepts refer to one thing, e.g., Ashoka is a tree. It is an inference in which there is no difference between the tree and the Ashoka—tree being the underly-ing point of reality. The Ashoka is existentially indentical with the tree. This relation is founded on identity, but identity is here not so much existential as conceptual. Here it is rooted in the very concept of Ashoka, which existentially involves also the concept of a tree.

A tree is produced from a seed. The relation is between the last moment of the seed and the first moment of the sprout. This relation between two realities, two under-lying point-instants, is causal, as one thing is produced from the other. It is the linking of two things (one of them is present and the other one was in the past) under one concept of casuality. It is a concept that involves relation. In this two things are placed under one concept. By analysing the concept of effect one can arrive at the concept of cause. By seeking the tree which is an effect, it is inferred that there must be something that caused it. Hence, from the effect we can infer the idea of the cause, which shows that the relation between cause and effect is logically necessary.

The main distinction between the relation of both is that in the first case two concepts are applied to one thing, whereas in the second case two things are placed under one concept.

The Buddhist philosophy goes deeper. According to the Buddhists, one entity does not produce or influence another entity out of itself. There is simple coordination between the moments following one another in an uninterrupted flux. There is neither duration nor any stabilized entity. The Buddhist idea of the concomitance of two things is that it represents an invariable and necessary bond.

The realistic ontology of the Buddhists required that some real relation must exist between the terms of the inference. It should be actual and knowable. The actual relation is that where one of the two things, so related, does not exist without the other.

Determination implies that a thing cannot be otherwise, and not that a thing is not otherwise. Only that leads the Buddhists to conclude that all inferences are necessary. Determination in the only condition which makes an inference valid. The inference can either be in the form of identity or causality, as it is between two concepts of one thing or one concept of two things, respectively. In both the cases it is a logically necessary relation.

The logical necessity is also imparted to the Buddhist theory of causality by the ontological standpoint. The whole system requires two entities, or two moments. The first is the cause which obviously leads to the second and thus causality is a consecution of discrete moments in an uninterrupted flux of reality.

Thus, the relation between cause and effect is a logically necessary relation according to the Buddhists. This makes their position just opposite of that of the non-Buddhists or the orthodox schools. The relation between cause and effect is contingent and not a logically necessary relation.

XXV

INTELLIGENCE

ABITS are conditions of intellectual efficiency. They operate upon intellect in two ways. They restrict its reach, they fix its boundaries. Outside the scope of habits, thought works gropingly. All habit forming involves the beginning of an intellectual specialization which, if unchecked, ends in thoughtless action. Fortunately, nature, which invites us to the path of least resistance, also puts obstacles in the way of our complete acceptance of its invitation. Even the most skilful aptitude bumps at times into the unexpected and gets into trouble, which only observation can solve.

Habit is a restriction of thought. Habits become negative limits because they are first positive agencies. The more numerous are our habits, the wider is the field of possible observation and foretelling. The doctrine of a single indissoluble soul was the cause of failure to recognise that concrete habits are the means of knowledge and thought. Concrete habits do all the perceiving and judging.

'Consciousness' expresses functions of habits, the phenomena of their formation, their operation and reorganization. Habits by themselves are too organized, too insistent to need inquiry. Impulses are too chaotic and confused to know.

Habit does incorporate or override objects, but it does not know them. Impulse scatters and obliterates them with its restless stir. The practical work done by habit and instinct in securing prompt and exact adjustment to the environment is not knowledge. A certain delicate combination of habit and impulse is requisite for observation, memory and judgment. Knowledge is not projected against the black unknown lives in the muscles but in the consciousness. Without habit there is only irritation and confused hesitation. With habit alone, there is a machine-like repetition. With conflict of habits and release of impulse, there is conscious search.

Whenever a conflict in habits is set up, an impulse is released. We strive to unify our responses to achieve a consistent environment which will restore unity of conduct.

Every habit is impulsive and urgent. The faculty of pure knowing enters a man from without as through a door. All knowing, judgment and belief represent an acquired result of the workings of nature of impulses in connection with environment. Impulse and habit are primary determinants of conduct.

The ends or objectives of conduct are those foreseen consequences which influence present deliberation and which finally bring it to rest by providing an adequate stimulus to overt action. They are terminals of deliberation and hence turning points in activity. The ends in view are ends or aims. They arise out of natural consequences which in the beginning are hit upon. While intelligence is confined to manipulation, it does not extend to construction. Generally our forecast of consequences is always subject to the bias of impulse and habit. We see what we want to see. We need those habits and dispositions which lead to impartial and consistent foresight of consequences. It is only then our judgments are reasonable and we are reasonable creatures.

What intelligence has to do in the service of impulse is to act not as its obedient servant but as its clarifier and liberator. Intelligence converts desire into systematic plans based on facts. Sometimes desire does not mean mere impulse but an impulse which has sense of an objective. Desire and thought cannot be opposed, for desire includes thought within itself.

The thought of an ideal is necessary to arouse dissatisfaction with the present and to arouse effort to change it. In reality the ideal is itself the product of discontent within existing conditions. When striving ceases, a moral holiday begins.

Happiness, reasonableness and virtue are parts of the present significance of a present action. Memory of the past, observation of the present, foresight of the future are very essential. Control of the future is precious in exact proportion to its difficulty and its degree of attainability. Forecast of future conditions and a scientific study of the past and present, in order that the forecast may be intelligent, are indeed necessities. Thought about future happenings is the only way to evaluate the present. But to subordinate the present deliberately to the future is to subject the comparatively secure to the precarious, i.e., to surrender what is under control to what is relatively incapable of control. Building a house is a typical instance of an intelligent activity. It is an activity directed by a plan. The plan is itself based upon a foresight of future uses. A man usually builds a house for comfort and security, the 'control' afforded to future living. Intellectual concern with the past and future is for the sake of directing the present activity. But we should keep in mind that the present activity is the only one really under our control. It is possible that the man may die before the house is built or his financial condition may change or he may need to shift to another place.

Thus, control of future living is wholly dependent upon taking the present activity seriously and devotedly: as an end, not as a means. Until people have formed the habit of using intelligence fully as a guide to the present action, they will never find out how much control of the future contingencies is possible. The realization of every activity resides in the present, made possible by judging the existing conditions. If education were conducted as a process of the fullest utilization of the present resources, liberating and guiding the capacities that are now urgent, it goes without saying that the lives of the young would be far richer in meaning than they are now.

In modern times the life of reason has been specialized or made a heavy burden. As a matter of fact, the present situation embodies the importance of the problem of activating the place of intelligence in conduct.

XXVI

SERVICE

TO take compassion on others is to treat them as phenomena in the world of phenomena. To love them, however, is to treat them as noumena. Man has to love man as his equal, both being members of the Kingdom of Ends. He has, therefore, to work for his own as well as other's perfection and only for happiness. To love is to serve; real love is sure to result in service. But the noblest form of such service is not rooted in the love for any individual but in the love for God. Man has to love man as God the universal man and not as man, a mere individual.

The highest endeavour of the mind and the highest virtue is to understand things by the third kind of knowledge or intuition. The mind's highest good is the knowledge of God and the mind's highest virtue is to know God. Such a kind of knowledge is love and so the highest virtue is the intellectual love of God. This love is the common bond between man and God and between man and man. God becomes the binding force. This is the basis of religion; the meaning of religion.

Love makes man see God everywhere. A mystic sees God in all beings and on all beings. A mystic who has realised God will love all men and naturally work for them.

Love radiates in him, it becomes his second nature to serve others, and leads to spiritual feedom. He looks on others as equal to himself.

A mystic's service is for all, universal empathy; he feels into the minds of others, identifies himself with them and serves them as if he would serve himself.

Real love takes a view which does not separate the part from the whole or the whole from the part. In self-contemplation, the noblest love that can be found on earth would disappear, for, none else than a real love can render selfless service and shower pure love. Some see more of the infinite wealth of the vision than others, but each receives according to the measure of his capacity.

Real love is a result of insight into the nature of ultimate reality. What is the difference between one and the other? When both are one, real service is possible only on the realisation of the divine nature of all. The difference between two individuals is that one serves, the other is different. On the ground, service becomes a possibility only in a fictionalistic fashion. With a fiction of the existence of the world all action becomes meaningful.

The ideal of service is realised only in God. God is the kindest of all for He alone can forgive His creatures and shower grace. Philosophers have tried to save the benevolence of God.

Such perfect service realised in God, of course, remains only an ideal. It is not found in experience. Nor is reason allowed to transgress the limits of experience and search for the ideal in the noumenal world. This noumenal world is not a duplicate world of ideas, it just shows the importance of reason to grasp by itself the totality of the ideal. The ideal may not be realisable in life, it may not be constitutive but it has an important regulative function of directing and systematising life. It remains an end term of a series to which experience continually approximates. We work selflessly as if this regulative ideal is one day going to be constitutive.

XXVII

FREEDOM OF MAN

EVERY civilization has its own aspirations and illusions, the dreams with which people are lulled to sleep and nightmares which do not allow them any rest. The words which are used to convey them have no static reference but shift their accent from generation to generation and from situation to situation. It has a political, religious and moral dimension. In time the emotional association may completely overwhelm its theoretical validity and its practical relevance. The modern mind has so succumbed to the lure of freedom that it cannot liberate itself from its bondage; the bondage which freedom has created. Man's life is a cosmic situation which is not of his doing but which leads to his undoing. Unless man is free to sin there cannot be any tragedy.

Freedom at the moral level is the freedom to act and at the same time the ability to go against the imperative of 'ought' and freely opt to do which "I ought not to": Freedom only to man who can do what he ought not to and not to the extra-terrestrial agents who cannot help being good. Freedom is irrevocably linked with human suffering. Freedom is liberation or deliverance from suffering and as such is possible here and now. One who has realized this on the earth has released himself from the cycles of birth and death and is nor subject to the tyranny of time and "the touch of the earthly years".

Freedom always points beyond itself to something without which it is not intelligible. Freedom revolts against any encroachment of its individualistic exclusiveness. It may overreach itself and may be construed as freedom from the state, and the state as such, by its very existence, may be deemed incompatible with the freedom of the individual. Freedom as freedom of the individual is an abstraction. The individual as an individual, in absolute isolation, is a myth and hence freedom has to take account of the individuals in their interrelational configuration. Freedom is possible only under restriction, or else the freedom of the individual, considered in a non-relational context, annuls freedom as such. The freedom of the individual is the concept of limitation which restricts its range, though it is a restriction which is accepted freely to make social existence possible.

Freedom has found its most vocal manifestation in the realm of expression. Rules and laws can create a formal framewok of art but artistic achievements have no worth without a creative element, an element of surprise or unpredictability. An artist has often claimed freedom from established norms without succeeding in establishing forms of expression and leaving as his achievements only oddities of expression and queer residues of unsuccessful experimentation. Art and social decorum have come into conflict and the whole idea of censorship is based on the belief that the aesthetic expressions are a part of social framework, and any deviation from social norms should be judged not by its aesthetic relevance but its social impact. But the artist has sometimes claimed not only freedom of expression and freedom to create novel patterns of beauty but, also, to lead a life in conformity with his artistic non-conformity. The life of the artist, however, is not part of his art. His life is to be judged in the context of the social framework obtaining in any given society.

225

Words are not really the static units of all language but the bearers of a dynamic process, conditioned by socio-historical change. The ability to use words is the human privilege to use symbols for communication and understanding. It is not man who has created language but it is language which has created man as the bearer of new values and qualities. Words create as much understanding as misunderstandings, as much reveal as 'conceal' what passes within the soul of man. Words which sway man take their sustenance from historical roots, and any attempt to plant them on a foreign soil leads to confusion for generations to come. Words may not be intended to reveal facts but as imperatives to give life to possibilities which have not yet attained any specific ontological status. Freedom may serve as a clarion call to radical changes, as an imperative to action.

Moral philosophy is the old problem of free will, the question whether man, in spite of all his apparent determinations from without, with all determinations of heredity and environment, still has the capacity to respond to the call of duty and defy all the irrational pressures and pulls which stand in the way of duty. This problem became all the more acute because without any freedom there cannot be any responsibility and without any responsibility moral life is emptied of its content. Man as an animal is held captive in the web of instinctual drives and desires. But he is more than an animal in so far as he can renounce what his nature craves for, and negate life as a system of desires for all that he considers to be more than life, and his capacity to negate and deny what life insistently demands. A religious person may consider even the earthly life a hindrance and may long to free himself from the restrictions of finite existence.

Anxiety is the urge to be free from all restrictions and pressures, from morality as an unwelcome legacy. Freedom is nothing short of the freedom from the transcendent. There is no alternative between the existence of God and human freedom and only in his metaphysical rootlessness, in his uncompromising loneliness, can man maintain his freedom. Man has bought his freedom at the cost of all that makes life worth living. But freedom does not mean loneliness or rootless segregation. It is the hidden desire for the distant, for something which has not yet come into being. The freedom of man is born of the anguish which involves as much disillusionment with the gods that failed as the yearning for the God who is yet to reveal Himself. Maybe, in this little world, 'freedom' has concealed the tragedy of man, his dissatisfaction with all that is, his mistrust of all that has been, and yet his attachment to life, as it unfolds itself here and now with its inadequacies and contradictions, too, is covered by it.

XXVIII

REASON

ANY talk about reason has to be reasonable. And, this fact at once reveals a very important aspect of the nature of reason. Reason does not permit any control from outside: it is self-controlled or autonomous. Let us assume that reason somehow gets its mandate sometimes from that which is not reason. In that case we shall have to admit, it is thought, that reason would become unreasonable. In other words, reason sets its own principles to follow. Let us examine this position a little closely.

We should try to find out under what conditions we can say that reason has become unreasonable. One point can be settled without much argumentation: it does not make any sense to talk of reason becoming unreasonable. No one says: "You are reasoning unreasonably." Rather, under those conditions, the apt statement would be: "You are unreasonable", "you are not talking rationally." This shows that either there is reason or there is none, but there is no possible position in between reason and unreason. This would, perhaps, set at rest the controversy centring around the notion of degrees of rationality.

Nothing would be reasonable to a certain degree, because that would imply that in other respects the same thing could also be unreasonable. The main argument in favour of this contention is that, the sphere of application remaining the same, you cannot attribute both rationality and its absence to it, and obviously this is a rule that reason has given us. This means that reason is not only self-controlled but it also distinguishes itself from a thing alien to it. In other words, reason chooses its own sphere of operation and, therefore, the sphere of the irrational is determined by reason itself and reason restrains itself from operating in that sphere.

Reason decides the sphere of its operation either on the ground of its inherent strength and weakness or because of its lack of awareness of its own capacity of operation. The first point is that reason is incapable of operating in the realm of things in themselves. The second point is the fact of gradual development of our knowledge. What was considered to be beyond reason, hence irrational, some time ago does become reasonable in course of time. What seems unreasonable, i.e., it is beyond the sphere of reason, today may well become reasonable, and hence included in the sphere of reason, tomorrow. And, it goes without saying that in this process reason also learns more and more of its own intricacies. Thus, reason is historical in the sense that its sphere goes on increasing. In this sense reason is also a self-enriching process, both in terms of its own functioning as well as in its sphere of operation.

It would be wrong to suppose that historicity makes reason personal. I may not know anything about quantum physics and I may not be able to talk reasonably regarding the behaviour of particles. But my incapacity to use reason in this case is due to my ignorance rather than due to lack of reason. From this we can draw two important conclusions: one, that the sphere of ignorance is not the sphere of reason; and two, because of historicity the standard of reason at any

229

given time is the general standard it has reached up to that time. Regarding the first point, ignorance is the state of absence of consciousness. In that state it is as much absurd to ascribe irrationality to it as it is to ascribe reason. Ignorance is not even the sphere of the irrational.

The distinction between reason and the irrational can be set by reason within the sphere of consciousness. I can apply reason to something else, of which, too, I am aware. In other words, reason sets its boundary somewhere within the domain of consciousness: what it leaves out, i.e., the irrational, has also to be within the same domain. The historicity of reason is significant because it brings out the impersonal character of reason. Reason accumulates information regarding its own mode of operation through the historical process of development and applies it in the course of its onward march. If this self-enriching process refers to individuals, it would have been impossible for any individual to understand another individual. If I have my own standard of reason, which you do not share with me, all my talk you might have liked to include in the sphere of the irrational, according to your idea of reason. What I am suggesting is that reason, though applied by individuals, is transpersonal, and displays the accumulated insight into the nature to reason up to a given time.

Conscious, impersonal, self-regulating reason sets its own boundary, and describes as irrational anything that is known to have been left outside this boundary. Paradoxically, you may say that reason determines the nature and domain of the irrational. But this should not be taken to mean that the irrational is also reasonable. Take, for instance, the case of a structure which allows contradictory elements in it. This structure would be called irrational not because reason permits contradiction but because reason refuses to either recognise this structure or it is prevented from operating in this case. In that case, the structure would be a going concern but it cannot claim a position along with any other structure that reason permits. Thus, the domain of the irrational is determined by reason in a negative sense: this domain is what reason has left out and not what reason has made. In this sense I take the irrational to be that domain where there is the possibility of the operation of reason, but reason has not yet cared to operate in it. One can always try to rationally understand the irrational, and there is no contradiction in saying that the irrational can be made rational by the application of reason.

The irrational has every possibility of becoming rational, and theoretically the domain of the irrational can become a part of the domain of reason. But, as pointed out earlier, any domain of reason, actual or possible, must be within the boundary of consciousness. This demands consideration of the relationship between reason and consciousness. Are the two, reason and consciousness, co-extensive or does one fall short of the other? To be sure, reason cannot cross the limits of consciousness. We find instances where in spite of consciousness reason cannot operate. For example, take the case of my awareness of my own existence. It is useless to ask, in this case, the question whether it is or it is not reasonable to have the awareness of my existence. But someone else may demand an explanation as to why this question is useless. And, obviously any explanation has to be reasonable. But here the demand is for the reasonability of my saying that reason is useless in cases like awareness of my existence. In other words, there is no need for any reason so far as my awareness of my existence is concerned, but there is a definite and legitimate demand for reason when I say that I do not need any reason for my awareness of my own existence. Who decides whether reason is needed or not needed in a particular instance? Well, if a decision is to come from a source other than reason, autonomous reason is bound to reject it. But if, on the other hand, it is the nature of reason itself that does not permit asking for reason for my not needing any reason for my awareness of my existence, then this would be the domain of consciousness where reason is not needed. This would not be the domain of the irrational because in the domain of the irrational it is always pertinent to ask for reason. Thus, the domain of the irrational is the possible domain of reason but such domain of consciousness where there is no demand for reason it would be the domain of the supra-rational.

The question of reason cannot be raised with regard to that state of consciousness. We can dispute statements about various states of consciousness, but we connot dispute our own particular state of consciousness where we ourselves do not feel the need of asking questions demanding reason. Any answer given in defence would base itself on the limit of reason. Since the veracity of reason is at stake, the incapacity of reason will be taken cautiously. But the fact remains that in states of direct awareness or feeling one has consciousness and in those states themselves there is no demand for reason. In this sense reason and consciousness are not co-extensive. Reason operates within a limited range of consciousness.

XXIX

PHENOMENON OF CHANGE

THE problem of change is very intimately connected with the problem of substance and quality or with the nature of material things. Common sense supposes that a substance or a thing exists in a three-dimension physical space, that a material object is to be defined by means of three properties, one of which is a 'position in space'. But this does not mean that a material object does not have a time dimension. Only, it is not a distinguishing characteristic of material things, since non-material (or mental) entities also have this characteristic in common with material things. It is only positive property by means of which we are able to define 'anything' that exists. But that a thing has a duration or a time dimension is either forgotten or ignored. This may lead to a belief that the thing is not of time, and, in fact, our language form supports such a belief. Even when we suppose that a thing is 'in time' we regard it to be different from time, related to it only by the relation 'in'. We regard the thing to be different from time precisely in the same way in which we regard a chair to be different from a table. Common sense believes that a substance or a thing has got spatial qualities, it does not believe that it has temporal qualities. The object or rather a thing is not merely that which we perceive at 'this moment'. What we know at 'this' moment is merely a section, a slice of a thing which occupies a section of time. 'This' denotes a specious present and not a real present. In fact, it is always necessary to specify the time at which a particular substance has the particular quality, and we rescue the reality. A substance has all the qualities which it possesses at any time during its existence, but it cannot have them all together.

If history is to be regarded as one thing, then, when two slices of the thing show a difference in character, we should not be able to say that the thing has changed. But, then, why are we able to say that there is a change? What is it that determines the individual identity of the thing? We are never aware of the whole history of the thing, or the whole thing. We are merely aware of some slice, smaller or bigger. Hence, we have an immediate experience of change but not of the identity of the thing. How can we decide that there is a thing up to a certain time and a thing after that? The question is, at what point does change become transformation, so that in undergoing the change the thing loses its identity?

It cannot be defined that we have a perception of change. If we mean by change a qualitative resemblance as well as qualitative difference between two slices of an enduring history, the concept of change can be significantly held.

There is no fixed measure or method by which we can determine the identity of a thing. A thing ceases to be regarded as the same when it suffers disruption — when it is broken up into parts, separate in space, so that each is thenceforth capable of having an independent history. When this happens, the thing no longer exists, but only its fragments do. Apart from this restriction, 'a material thing may always be regarded as maintaining its identity through change'.

So long as the unity and continuity of our interest in the thing is unbroken, it remains for us the same thing. Suppose

234

a lump of iron-ore is taken out of the mine it does not matter to us if it is separated into two parts, and out of one a typewriter is made while out of the other a 'tank' is manufactured. We will be interested in the histories of the tank and the typewriter only so far as both of them together make the history of the iron lump, and these two articles separated in space will still form part of the same iron-ore. If the typewriter and the tank are remelted and formed in one lump, still the lump will add to the history of the iron lump. On the other hand, if we are interested only in the typewriter, we will find that the typewriter loses its identity if we go either to its past history, when it was a part of the iron lump, or to its future history, when it would be melted as scrap. We then conclude that, though we know that a thing must have a duration or history, what exactly is the life of a thing depends on our purposive interest.

Change is the only reality, and there is nothing immutable in the universe. All entities which are in time have a duration, they persist and in that they change. So, if there are any entities which do not change they must be beyond time. These must be such that we should not be able to say that they are in time. The ideas or what we call universals, not being particular, cannot exist in the world of sense, or time. Take such a notion as justice or whiteness. In experience we shall never meet with such general notions. We shall meet with some just act or some shade of white colour. But the common nature, so it is thought, by virtue of which all acts are just will be justice itself, and the common nature by virtue of which all shades of white will be white is whiteness itself. The particulars perish, but the universals remain constant. Now these universals, it can very easily be seen, do not change. For had a universal changed with a particular, then, as soon as a particular perished, the universal would have been no more and we would not have been able to refer to it when we come across another particular. If we make a judgement, 'this flower is white' and if the universals are not constant, we should not be able to say that another flower is white, or the wall is white. Even if it is said that this particular colour is different from that partcular colour, we at least find a similarity between the two and the phenomenon of similarity cannot be explained without recognising a universal. If universals are not immutable and still are in some way different from the particulars, the universal whiteness would perish as soon as the white flower perished. Universals are not in time but are eternal, i.e., existing for all time. Universals can 'exist' in time only through particulars. But, if the particulars are annihilated, the notion of universals still persists. Mammoths do not exist now. But the concept of mammothhood is not destroyed. Thus, it appears that temporary predicates are irrelevant for universals. There are three senses in which the word 'permanent' is used. By permanent is meant that which is in time but persists for all times, i.e., eternal; that which is relatively permanent and that which is out of time, i.e., timeless.

The concept of change is complex. There cannot be change useless there is something different at one time from what there is at another. Change must involve relations and complexity, and must demand analysis. So long as our analysis has only gone as far as other smaller change, it is not complete; if it is to be complete, it must end with terms that are not changes, but are related by a relation of earlier and later: the conception of instants without duration, or at any rate without any duration which even the most delicate instruments can reveal. Change always involves a fixed entity and a three-cornered relation between this entity, another entity and some, but not all, the moments of time.

In change there should be two states of an entity at different times. Change is analyseable into instants without duration, related to each other by the relation of 'earlier than' and 'later than'.

Can we formulate the idea of artificially joining durationless instants by the relation of 'earlier than' and 'later than'? If we cannot, there must be something wrong in the starting point itself. It is true that wherever there exists a relation of 'earlier than' and 'later than', there is change. The relation of 'earlier than' and 'later than' presupposes past, present and future, and these again presuppose duration. It is the characteristic of being the past, present and future that is necessary for change. It follows that because the relations of 'earlier than' and 'later than' are derived from 'a serial of characteristics like the past, present and future,' the concept of change gives significance to the relations of 'earlier than' and 'later than'. Thus, the concept of change is logically prior to the relations of earlier and later.

The concept of change does not admit analysis because the very conception which is to be analysed is involved in some part of the analysis, or it is the analysis of an altogether different entity. It is only because the concept of change is unanalyseable that we cannot give an analytical definiton of the concept but have to describe it in relation to a certain situation. Change should be regarded as a unique and simple portion.

Change must be in time. It must imply time. Is there time without change? Can time be a static medium? But time itself is a kind of flow, and it must change. Time implies change. Change and time are co-implicates. Change is not distinguishable from time. Time can be distinguished from change only if we begin to talk of time in a mathematical sense. Change and time cannot be distinguished.

Then there is the relation of space to change. Many changes are in space, and presuppose space. When there is

237

a change of a physical object, it necessarily presupposes the existence of space. 'Motion' which is only a kind of change must necessarily take place in space. For example, the phenomenon of a moving train. What has changed here? Has the train changed simply because formerly it was in one position and is now in another? Many, and perhaps most, people would answer that the train has not changed. What has changed then? It is the relation which the train had with space and time that has changed. So the change consists in the relation of the train to space-time-field, and such a kind of change does presuppose space.

Change seems to be impossible without time, so change does not seem to be impossible without space. When we hear some music and 'feel' a change, the change is not spatial, though, indeed, so far as the sounds are sound waves, the change may be regarded as spatial.